# 44 Baseball Mistakes & Corrections

*For the Youth Baseball Parent/Coach*

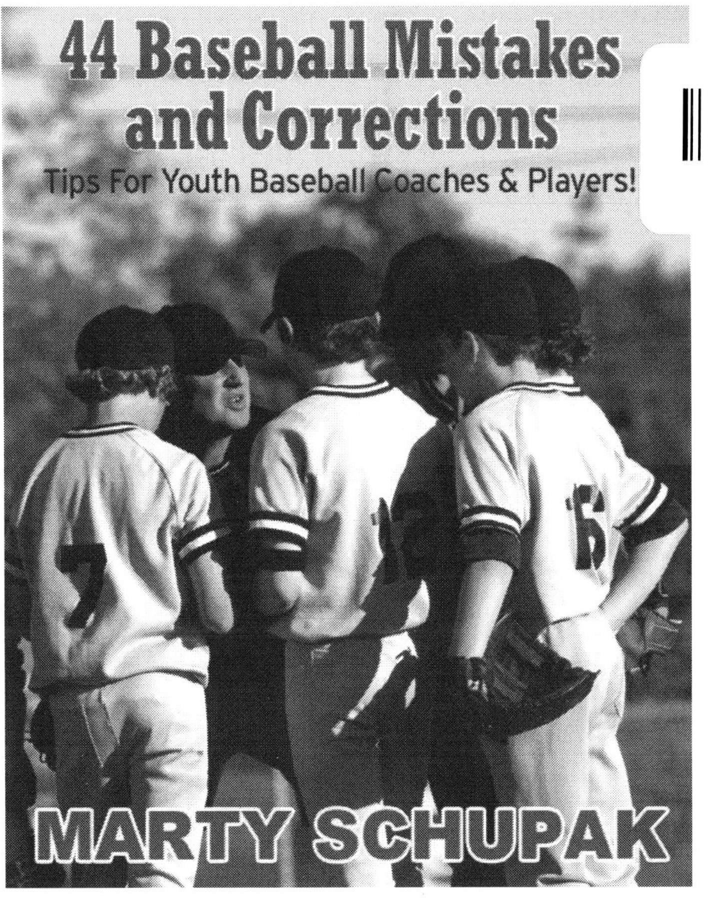




By Marty Schupak
*First Edition*

TABLE OF CONTENTS

# 44 Baseball Mistakes & Corrections

Youth Sports Club, Inc.

9 Florence Court

Valley Cottage, NY 10989



To order copies, call 845-536-4278.

*This book is dedicated to my wife Elaine.*

*Thanks for your unending support!*

## *Chapter 1*

# Introduction

*"Baseball is like church. Many attend few understand"*
*-Leo Durocher*

Wouldn't life be different if we knew things in advance before they ever happened?

When we were all in high school, the SAT test played a huge part of our lives if we planned to go to college. Now imagine getting the SAT questions ahead of time for the test. You'd probably score better than you did. And this might have changed your future, maybe by getting into a college. Or even going to a better college than you thought was possible. Now imagine you are negotiating to buy your first house or condominium. The negotiating is going back and forth. All you know is you and your spouse want this home. Suppose you were able to read the minds of the sellers? You'd no doubt get the house or condominium at a better price than you normally would.

Throughout my 25 years coaching baseball I didn't have to be Casey Stengel or Earl Weaver to notice that kids 10, 11, and 12 years-old would make the same mistakes as other players would make. These mistakes would happen over and over again. I began taking note of these mistakes and made a concerted effort to practice rectifying many of them by putting my players and team in a position to succeed. The two examples I mentioned above are related in that when my team and I knew what was going to happen during the course of the season, we were prepared. But, we were prepared only because we practiced and practiced situational baseball. If some of the situations did not happen that year, so what! I was not just preparing the team for the present season but wanted to prepare them to become better baseball players for as long as they played or followed the game of baseball.

Every year some of my outfielders would hold the ball too long, not knowing which base to throw it to. I came up with a way to resolve this issue. The first few years coaching, I didn't know the difference between interference and obstruction.

With this, I came up with a way for both my players and myself to understand the differences. These two, and forty-two other mistakes are reviewed in this book, giving you the coach and/or parent the method to overcome each one. There are no doubt more than forty-four mistakes that come up each and every year but I have taken what I think are the top mistakes. The way I usually work is when I have been burned, and burned bad, by a certain mistake, I get obsessed with getting it right. So when you read through this book you will already know that coach Marty Schupak and his team were burned one or more times by each mistake. Of course even when you have your team practice how to correct a mistake, there is no guarantee it will be corrected if the situation occurs in a game. What we want to do as youth coaches and parents is to put the odds in our favor to succeed. Like an NFL coaching staff developing a game plan for their upcoming game, we coaches want to prepare our young players for almost everything.

The one thing I want to emphasize is not to overwhelm the kids with too much teaching at one time. Remember that most kids at this age can only absorb a certain amount of information at once. If we feed the players with too much at one time it will become counter productive and be more confusing than clear. However long your baseball season is, pick a few mistakes to go over at each practice. Reinforce them in subsequent practices while introducing new mistakes and their remedies. And remember to develop your own coaching style. It is okay to take bits and pieces from your old high school or youth league coach but when you develop your own style, you will get more mileage from your coaching than if you copied only one person and tried to imitate that person every way he does things.

I have written this book in a way that I would like to read it if I were a brand new or experienced coach. For every one of the forty-four mistakes I write about, I've tried to inject real game situations that have happened to me or that I observed. I have found that if you can picture the situation in your head, it will be more practical. I also highly recommend you view my video of the same name:

<u>44 Baseball Mistakes & Corrections</u>

The visual (which should be at your local library) will be most helpful, and you can share it with your team. When I do my coach's clinics around the country, one of the things I stress to new and experienced coaches is you have two ways of teaching your team techniques and skills during the season. You can tell them what to do and describe how to do it or you can tell your team what to do and then show them in practice how to do it. Here is an example. I hear many coaches tell a player who gets to third base with less than two outs that if there is a fly ball to the outfield, stay on the base to tag up. There is no need to take a lead. This is true, but wouldn't it be better if each player in practice did this live first, so in the game it would become almost second nature?

My remedies are subjective. If you can find remedies that players will understand better, please use them. In all the videos and books I have authored, my main goal is to ignite the creative juices in the mind of all coaches and parents who love the sport of baseball and youth sports in general. When you get involved in youth sports with your son or daughter, the clock keeps ticking and the experience with your kids during this time will give you the best memories you will ever have. The bonding you will develop with your own kids and others in your community will last a lot longer than you realize.

Play hard and fair and remember, improve as individuals, improve as a team and have fun!

*Chapter 2*

# Mistake #1

## Not Warming Up The Team

I remember going to my podiatrist about an issue I had with my foot. We began talking about jogging. As it turns out we both used the same route a few days a week for our jogs. A local park with a great 3.1-mile trail around a lake was extremely popular for the locals. The doctor would go on to tell how when he jogged around the lake he took special notice of the different people who were getting ready to jog. Did they warm up, and if so, did they do so properly? He would make mental notes, telling himself which ones would end up in his office just because of the way they were warming up. No doubt he was probably right, and a good part of his practice was busy with patients who neglected to warm-up correctly, or didn't do anything and paid the price later on.

With young kids, warming up is just as important. Many coaches don't think it is necessary for young kids to take the time to warm-up. Remember the adage, "Warm-up to throw, Don't throw to warm-up." I used to be 100% guilty of not taking the time to have my team warm-up before a practice or a game. Especially when I coached the really young kids. I never thought that warming up for say, 7 or 8 year olds would make any kind of difference. I was wrong. I have read numerous studies over the years and have followed the writings of some well known orthopedic sports doctors. To a person, each of these doctors have stated you need to warm up your players. Even the very young players. Studies have shown that warming up will help prevent injuries in the long run. Warm-ups from 10-20 minutes (or longer) seem to be the recommended time. But, even a very short warm-up between 3-5 minutes can be effective. Warming up can have a few benefits. It can help to prevent injuries and it can help to enhance performance for the athlete. Another benefit that I think is overlooked is that having young players warm-up is getting them into good habits at an early age. So for coaches of youth players, please take the time to warm-up your team. You need not be an athletic trainer with intricate exercises. You can speak to your local high school trainer and ask him or her for 5-10 warm-up drills. Many times your local league will have a warm-up routine that was put together by either a local person or by the national home office of the league you are associated with.

Some leagues even have a local orthopedic doctor address the league coaches before the start of the season. How ever you get a warm-up program doesn't matter all too much. The important thing is to do the warm-up.

Many times we would start our warm-up with a jog around the outfield grass. And if you are in shape (and see a doctor. before you do it) it is a good idea for coaches to jog with the kids.

After our lap we would line up in a straight line and do arm rotations. We would first do the left arm rotating going forward, then going backward. Then the other arm. And finally both arms together. We would then do the basic jumping jacks a number of times. Then we would do "body twists." Staying in one spot with hands on the hips moving from left to right and back again. We would then go back to the arms and do a little resistance exercise. With the arm in about a 45-degree angle, each player would hold his own elbow while pressing down with the free hand giving resistance as the players try to push their elbow down. We would do this a few times.

After this we would practice pitching with the full wind-up without the baseball. Everybody is a pitcher in this drill and we continue to do this 4-6 times. All this takes about 5-7 minutes and the kids get used to it. Appointing a "warm-up captain" can be a good idea. But keep in mind some kids are incredibly uncomfortable in front of their teammates.

I mentioned having your players take a jog around the field first before you do anything. I'd like to philosophize a little bit about running. If you played high school sports like myself, running has almost always been looked at as a punishment. This negative connotation remains with the kids. I want to challenge you coaches and parents out there. How about we turn this around. For young athletes, let's use running as a reward instead of a punishment. When your team does something good, let's reward them and have them do a victory lap around the field.

If this changes only a few of the kids ideas about running, maybe we as youth coaches can help with the ever growing obesity problem our society is having. We must teach our youth to change their thinking about running and exercise.

When it comes to having your youth team warm up, as coaches and parents, we must strive to do the right things at an early age. Having your team warm up is a must, even for the younger ones. As I mentioned, everything is right when you get kids into good habits at a young age.

**Related Resources:**

44 Baseball Mistakes & Corrections

Baseball Coaching: A Guide for the Youth Coach & Parent

*Chapter 3*

# Mistake #2

## Using Gloves That Are Too Big

If you are a baseball historian who loves old baseball film footage, like I do, you will see that once the game started players would never bring their gloves into the dugout as long as they were in the game. The tradition lasted up until the 1950's. After the third out was made, the fielders would leave their gloves on the field. The way people buy and work in gloves has changed over the years and in turn changed the tradition. This, and the cost of some of the gloves on the market right now would shock baseball players from the 1920's and 30's.

I have found that the size of baseball gloves has always been an issue, especially with parents. When I was a youngster, I was fortunate that I lived on a block that played sports each and every day of the year no matter what the weather conditions were. All the kids were sports-orientated and even the young brothers were included in most games. I'm a lefty and there was only one other lefty who lived on our street. His name was Peter, who was three years older than me. I was lucky that whenever Peter grew out of his glove, I would inherit his lefty mitt. If his brother Mark was lefty, I probably would not have been the beneficiary, but it worked out for me. This situation gave me a few advantages. I didn't have to bother my parents to buy a new glove all the time. And, unlike my friends, who did get new gloves, I didn't have to break them in. Peter had done this by using it for a few years before he gave it to me. It turned out to be a great opportunity for me.

A number of years ago I was fortunate to be invited to go to a baseball game at Yankee Stadium and had front row seats between 3rd base and home. This was the first time (and probably the last) that I will ever get close to those seats again. A bonus was that one of the people who invited me was a friend of the second baseman of the Yankees. After doing some of his warm-up drills he had a free moment and came over to acknowledge his friend and spoke with us for a few minutes. While we were conversing, I took notice of his glove. Being a second baseman I knew the glove could not be too big. But I was stunned at how small the glove actually was. In fact, I would swear that the glove was almost an exact outline of his hand. It was a learning moment for myself, who was just getting into coaching.

My oldest son loved baseball. We were both excited when I bought him his first baseball glove. I remember looking forward to working the glove in just like my dad helped me do the few times we bought a glove instead of getting one from my neighbor, Peter. When my dad got me my first glove, we used an oil to rub in it with a rag and put two baseballs in it and tied string around it. Every moment I had I would untie the string and throw a baseball into it and repeat this hundreds of times before wrapping the string around it before putting it to sleep. With my son's glove, we did the appropriate treatment and he worked it in the same way I did. Now here is the mistake I made and so do many other parents. I attributed buying baseball gloves the same way we buy shoes for our kids as their feet grow. Every time I bought a new glove, I got one bigger than the last one. You do not need to buy a new glove for your kids every year or every other year. And you do not need a bigger glove each and every time you purchase one. You want your kids to have a glove they can control and catch the baseball comfortably. If the glove is too big, many times the player won't be able to feel the ball going into it and may not instinctively close the glove to secure the baseball. This will hurt the player's fielding performance. The experience I had seeing the Yankee second baseman's glove was one of the best educations with gloves I ever had.

I located a chart that many people adhere to when purchasing a glove for their kids. Remember that certain leagues will have size limitations, so find out what sizes are acceptable. Here is some recommended sizes:

Age 8 and Under: 9 to 11 Inches

Age 9 to 13: 10 to 12 Inches

Age 13 to 18: 11 to 13 Inches

To me the recommended correct size is the size that works. Some more details

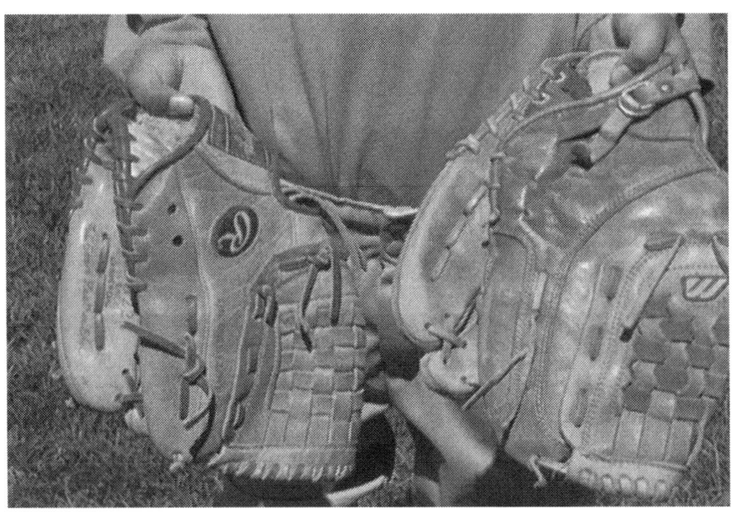

about baseball gloves are the material. There are three basic types of baseball glove materials: cowhide, pigskin and synthetics. To me it doesn't matter what the material is as long as it works.

I personally think what people pay for baseball gloves and bats are almost obscene. Let me give you a hint that I have used before and that has worked for many families. In your neighborhood, locate one or two families that have older kids who may be in college, or even graduated college. On a Sunday afternoon, walk over with your kids and ring the bell. Introduce yourself as a neighborhood family and that you know the children in the house have grown and if they are interested in getting rid of some old baseball equipment. More often than not you

will walk away with some excellent worked in baseball goods. If you get the woman of the house, she will lay down a red carpet and take you into the garage or basement and give you anything you want.

Another hint. If your son is a catcher, try to get one that is broken in already. I always advise leagues for teams to have a new glove each year that is their practice catcher's glove and it is up to that team to use it in practice working it in for next year's team.

In summing up, make sure when you purchase your son or daughter's gloves, they are big enough to control, but not too big. Remember when talking about baseball gloves, bigger is not always better.

**Related Resources:**

44 Baseball Mistakes & Corrections

Baseball Coaching: A Guide for the Youth Coach & Parent

Fielding Drills & Techniques

*Chapter 4*

# Mistake #3
## Catching Everything With 2 Hands

I have been fortunate to have known a lot of coaches in all sports. I was attending a high school playoff basketball game that was going down to the wire. The team of the coach I knew was down by one point at the end of the game. With a few seconds left, one of the guards got some space and drove all the way down the left side of the basket and put in a lay-up with his right hand, just out of the reach of two defenders. The team won the game. Later that week I ran into the coach and congratulated him on the team's great victory. I couldn't help asking him why the guard didn't take the lay-up lefty since he was on the left side. The coach explained that the guard, who was a righty, was most comfortable with his strong hand. He explained that he teaches his team the correct fundamentals with lefty and righty lay-ups, however always emphasizes that his players shoot with the hand that will make the basket.

This conversation stuck with me.

In baseball, each and every fielding play is slightly different from the one before. I know some people will vehemently disagree with me but I don't recommend trying to catch every ball with two hands. I would say in almost every book on baseball fundamentals you will read that you have to teach kids to catch everything with two hands. I think this is 100% wrong. As a coach, I want my players to catch a ball any way they can. I want them to practice catching a ball with two hands. I also want them practicing catching a ball with one hand. Let me explain my reasoning on this.

Before I give you my explanation I want to urge all new youth coaches to use soft covered balls to start when teaching catching fundamentals. I'm a big believer in using props, different size balls, or even Scatch balls with a Velcro paddle and Velcro ball to help kids gain confidence catching a baseball. The worst thing we can do for young players is throw a hard ball at them at their first practice and they get hit in the face or nose and never want to step on the baseball field again. We want to instill confidence in young players so they keep coming back every year to play. With very young t-ball players I recommend what I call the "progression method." As a lead up to catching a ball, have the younger players just make contact with the ball And not try to catch it. This will pay dividends for the younger players, Then they can build up to catching the baseball. When the fielding practice gets more advanced, it is beneficial to get the players used to moving their feet instead of just reaching for the baseball with their hand.

Back to one-handed and two-handed catches. Most of the time in baseball and youth baseball a ball could and should be caught with two hands. There are times though when it is easier for a player to catch the baseball with one hand rather than both hands. When catching a pop-up hit right to a player, with little or no running, a two-handed catch works best. Too many coaches and parents overemphasize catching everything with two hands. The simple fact is there are a lot of baseballs that are not hit right at a player. He may have to move multiple steps to his right or his left. Imagine a shortstop sprinting fast into foul territory behind third base trying to catch a foul ball. The only way he can make the play is if he stretches out his glove arm toward the baseball that is descending toward the ground very fast. I maintain that on a play like this it is virtually impossible for the fielder to make the play if he has to do so with two hands. If your center fielder is running in a sprinter's mode trying to make a catch, two hands are a tough way to do it. Imagine a shoe string two-handed catch? I don't think I ever saw one. Coaches must be flexible the way they teach the game of baseball. They should teach their players to be flexible by coaching flexible. As a coach I urge all other coaches and parents to teach their kids to catch with both two hands and with one hand. This is for ground balls as well as fly balls. A good rule is that two hands should be used in most cases when your body is completely behind the ball. But, when a player is moving fairly quickly it will probably be easier for him to catch the ball with one hand. The bottom line is to teach the correct fundamentals with one and two handed catches, but teach players to catch the baseball anyway they can. A very important point for coaches is to not berate kids if they use one hand and make the catch.

The best coaches in any sport at any level are the ones that show flexibility. Coaches that are able to change and think outside the box are the most successful. Teach your kids to catch the ball with both one and two hands. They will become better players!

**Related Resources:**

44 Baseball Mistakes & Corrections

Baseball Coaching: A Guide for the Youth Coach & Parent

Fielding Drills & Techniques

Infield Team Play & Strategies

*Chapter 5*

# Mistake #4
## Holding Ready Position Too Long

When we coach young players we have to realize there is always a conflict whenever we teach a skill. For instance, the coach must ask himself in teaching this skill is the concentration span of all 12 kids able to grasp the concept and skill? The attention span of today's youth is being challenged more and more. My wife, who is in the education field, tells me this all the time and we both agree the situation is getting worse. Kids have an overflow of information being thrown at them all fighting for their attention. Because of the times we live in, kids have a tremendous amount of access to information. There have been statistical studies that show the average attention span is down from 12 seconds to 8.25 seconds according to the National Center for Biotechnology Information and the U.S. National Library of Medicine. Coaches and parents have to realize that kids are asked to absorb more information today in a shorter period of time. 1

I developed my own coaching philosophy that confronts the short attention span of kids today head on. I realized the best way to teach sports skills is to keep my practices short, upbeat, and integrate fun drills with skill drills. All my baseball practices would run anywhere from 60-90 minutes with multiple drills. It is important to have structure, but it is just as important to let your players be kids. This has worked for me for twenty-five years. I mentioned how youth coaches have to show flexibility. When it comes to coaching youth athletes I learned that some techniques and drills that work with one group will not work with another group the next year. Coaches always have to be thinking about alternate ways to teach techniques and drills. I remember one year I had instilled three defensive plays for first and third situations.We did incredibly well that year defending and even getting double plays. I thought I had discovered a magic bullet, only to find out the next year my infielders could not grasp the same defensive plays even with half of the same infield. I then came to the conclusion that my catcher from the year before was the best one I ever had and he was the key to defending the steal situation. It was more the catcher than it was my coaching. I had to show flexibility and put in defensive plays according to the talent of my team.

In baseball, we always want our fielders to be in the "ready position", feet spread apart, knees bent with the glove and free hand out in front of the player.

Some coaches have their own variation, like taking one or two steps forward, but the point is to have your defense ready on the pitch. Whether it is a line drive or a hit to either side and the player has to move. This is the first step to making a defensive play. Whatever you teach your players, I highly encourage you to teach your players to time it when they get into the ready position. Here is my point. If we agree that young kids have a limited attention span then shouldn't we time when the players should get ready? Don't we want them at optimum position to make the play? I recommend you teach your kids to get into the ready position when the pitcher begins his wind-up. This gives ample time, somewhere in the 2-3 second range for the players to "get ready." I have seen coaches tell their fielders to get in the ready position and then he instructs the pitcher to tie his shoes.

The players remain stoic, concentrating for maybe 25-35 seconds. Kids cannot hold it for that long. So remedy the mistake many coaches make. Time your team's "ready position" and coincide it with the pitcher's wind-up. The players will be ready to field and it works!

Here's another hint when talking about attention spans. I had a player a number of years ago, Mike, who was a difficult kid to coach. He had ability, but his mind would always wander. When I had him in the outfield, a fly ball hit to him would sometimes drop right near him. It seemed sometimes he wouldn't even know the ball was hit. I tried him at catcher one game and he was a different player. He was scorching the ball as a hitter and his athletic ability really came together as a defensive catcher. I realized that he had some kind of attention deficit. By putting him in as catcher, there was a play on every pitch, forcing him to be a different player. It was amazing to watch a caterpillar turn into a butterfly.

Every kid is different. Each will need different ways to motivate them. Some kids just hate it if a coach or teacher raises their voice at them. Others will respond to a little bit of yelling. We are youth coaches and not psychologists, but if you get to know your team and your players, you will learn what works and what doesn't work. You will also see as you continue to coach youth sports that this will carry over into other sports if you get some of the same kids on your team.

1 From the Internet: Coaching Kids With A Short Attention Span

**Related Resources:**

44 Baseball Mistakes & Corrections

Baseball Coaching: A Guide for the Youth Coach & Parent

Fielding Drills & Techniques

Infield Team Play & Strategies

Winning Baseball Strategies

*Chapter 6*

# Mistake #5
## Fielding Ground Balls Under Legs

In my quest as a sports parent with two boys and one girl, I was always seeking the next best sports activity that was doable in my backyard. My love was to create sports activities and drills that I could involve my kids. I remember creating the bubble drill. When my kids were two or three years old I would get one of those big red bats and blow bubbles all over my backyard. The goal was to hit and burst the bubbles. I would do this for what seemed like hours with each of my kids, who couldn't get enough of this fun activity. Each would run all over my backyard swinging this big red bat. There were no style points or technique here. Just bust the bubbles. It was awesome! Many other drills I tried didn't appeal to my kids but with one, I hit the jackpot. This drill was called the "dive drill". I would put two cones about ten feet apart in an area in my backyard with thick grass. I would roll the ball, at first underhanded, and my son(s) or daughter would have to dive with their baseball glove on and try not to let the ball get by them. I remember yelling out to them "move your feet, move your feet." I didn't realize it then, but this drill and variations of it would become a huge repertoire of my practices. Teaching players to move their feet will help with teaching kids the correct way to field ground balls.

In my twenty-five years coaching kids it's funny how they use their energy. If you leave them alone, they will play for hours on end. But sometimes if you have something structured, kids will take the easy way out. Not on purpose, but just instinctively. Here is an example. If a ground ball is hit to a young baseball player to either his left side or his right side, many times certain players will reach for the ball rather than moving their feet to get in front of the ground ball. Young players can get lazy without even knowing it. That is why practice is important. If you run players through drills with the proper fundamentals, the muscle memory will record this, and in a live game, it will be second nature. Even with young players.

I have said it before. When you are teaching any fielding techniques, I recommend the use of soft covered baseballs. This is the way to go with young players and the best way to prevent injuries. I've heard some "macho" coaches state that it is okay for even young players to get whacked with the ball a few times to ensure they learn from it and do it right. If you do this, the soccer coaches in your area will love you. Players that get hurt in baseball at a young age very often leave the sport for good. They'll end up playing another sport.

Many times youth players will catch a ground ball underneath their body letting it go too deep. Of course the player can still make the out but our job it to teach the correct fundamentals to have the player in the best position to succeed. When one aspect of the fundamentals is thrown off, this can affect other parts of the play. For instance if the ball is fielded too far under the player's body, this may lead to a bad throw to first base. We want our players to get it right from beginning to the end of the play. When you teach catching the grounder in front of the player, point out the triangle that is formed with both feet when the ball goes into the glove.

When the player is not catching the baseball in front of him, he could be bending with his knees or back, but not both. When you catch the ball too deep, you are losing the "soft hands" advantage. The term "soft hands" perfectly describes how the hands should be. Both the glove hand and the throwing hand should be relaxed. When the player gets older he will learn to make last second adjustments on bad hops. Fielding the baseball under the body will impede these last second adjustments. I have also heard coaches say that the glove and free hand should be in front of the bill of the cap. If this works with your players, use it!

It is just as important for young players in the outfield to field ground balls coming to them the same way. I've seen too many times how the outfielder can become anxious listening to coaches and parents shouting, trying to hurry the process up. The players will lift their glove up too soon. The ball then goes through their legs and then there are extra bases for the baserunners. It is just as important for coaches to practice fielding ground balls in the outfield as well as the infield.

There are numerous aspects when catching a ground ball. Fielding the ball in front of the player is giving him the best chance to make the play. I've used this before, but parents and coaches should not "over coach and under teach." A team with twelve young players on it will not absorb everything equally. Coaches and parents have to tweak the way to teach some fundamentals. Some teaching techniques will work for some and not for others. Coaches and parents have to keep their flexibility. Teach your players to field the ground ball in front of them and do it the best way your team will understand it!

**Related Resources:**

44 Baseball Mistakes & Corrections

Baseball Coaching: A Guide for the Youth Coach & Parent

Fielding Drills & Techniques

The 59 Minute Baseball Practice

Baseball Chronicles: Articles On Youth Coaching

*Chapter 7*

# Mistake #6
## Teams Not Teaching Or Practicing Interference

It is incredible how some coaches know the rules inside and out. I am a huge NFL fan. If you follow the New England Patriots legendary head coach Bill Belichick it is amazing at how well he knows the rules of the game. He learns the rules and figures out how to get an edge from these rules. He is so adept at this that the NFL actually changed a rule because he found an advantage during a game. Being a lifelong New York Jets fan he has driven me crazy. Coaches at the youth level never really master the rules like a Belichick does, but they should become familiar with the rules The short story I'm about to tell really has nothing to do with interference but it has something to do with not knowing the rules. A number of years ago my team was in the playoffs. We were involved in a really close one run game. Very late in the game, we had a runner on third with one out. My batter attempted to bunt on the first two pitches and missed. He was down in the count 0-2. I decided to take a chance, like I've done before, and I gave the batter the bunt sign with two strikes. Not a popular decision in baseball 101. The pitcher pitched the ball and my batter got into the "square bunt" position, as opposed to the "pivot bunt." He laid down the most beautiful bunt down the third base line that hugged the foul line in fair territory. The ball died at the perfect spot. For a second, I felt like a genius knowing the runner from third would score and we'd have another baserunner. To my surprise, before I had time to pat myself on the back, the home plate umpire called my batter out.

Apparently he stepped on home plate with his right foot while he was squared to bunt and the ball made contact with the bat. I was stunned and tried to give a convincing argument, but it remained an out and we ended up being eliminated from the playoffs. Now, this story has nothing to do with interference, but even for 10, 11 and 12 year-old kids, if I took 5 minutes some time during the season and explained about stepping on home plate, maybe we would have went further in the playoffs. You can bet your bottom dollar that every year since I explain to my team about bunting and making contact with home plate.

Better yet, I show them on the field about stepping on home plate while making contact with the baseball.

It must have been two or three years into my baseball coaching career that I realized I did not know the difference between interference and obstruction. I do know in the course of that time some of the young umpires that I saw do games did not know the difference either. In baseball, interference occurs in situations in which a person illegally changes the course of play. Interference can be committed by various ways. There can be interference by players on the offense, players not currently in the game, catchers, umpires, and even spectators. Each type of interference is covered differently by the rules. Since I learned the difference between interference and obstruction I have seen coaches and/or parents yell from the dugout or stands "interference" when it is "obstruction" and "obstruction" when it is "interference." I have been burned as a coach by both interference and "obstruction". Each and every year we go over both in practice, teaching our players the difference. It is the best interest for your team to go over each of these terms. As teachers, it is always much better to show your players than it is to just tell them. You can teach this by age group. The really young kids might not all grasp it, but when you are coaching 10,11 and 12 year-olds, explain and set up different situations to show them.

The most common type of interference usually refers to an act by the offensive team that impacts the defense making a play. Think in terms of a baserunner running from second to third, bumping the shortstop as the ball is coming to him. I see interference also happen when baserunners either are watching the baseball when they shouldn't be or making extra wide turns around the bases. In both of these cases, the baserunner will sometimes bump a fielder involved in a play.

Obstruction refers to a fielder who hinders a runner. Quite simply, interference is a 'penalty' against the offense, and obstruction is a penalty against the defense.

Coaches must spend time teaching how our baserunners should avoid a collision with a fielder. If a collision is imminent, it is up to the baserunner to stop or run around the fielder while remaining in the baseline.

As coaches, don't get too obsessed with this. I usually spend 10-15 minutes in one practice going over "interference" situations on all the base paths. At times I have supplemented teaching this on the field with handouts showing one or two situations. Spending this time going over it and reinforcing the concept throughout the season may save you a run or even a playoff game.

**Related Resources:**

44 Baseball Mistakes & Corrections

Baseball Coaching: A Guide for the Youth Coach & Parent

Baserunning & Bunting Drills

*Chapter 8*

# Mistake #7

## Not Practicing Obstruction

I have followed sports my whole life. I have been fortunate to witness in person or on television some of the most historical games played in the last fifty years. I have always thought it almost amazing when a hit, basketball shot, or long pass in football occurs that the officials or umpires are able to watch the game away from where the ball, hit, or action is occurring. In youth sports many times the officials who are not as experienced as the professionals on television will be watching the action when they should be watching another part of the field. The reason I mention this is because a lot of times when "obstruction" occurs, it happens nowhere near where the action of the baseball game is taking place. This could be frustrating for a Little League coach who knows many of the rules of the game, and because of the nature of the league, there may be only one umpire. It will be impossible to see the whole field.

When baseball began and it was gaining traction popularity with the public, the rules makers were observing the game and tried feverishly to install positive changes. It is said that Alexander Cartwright wrote the first set of baseball rules in 1845.

These rules were called the Knickerbocker Rules. This has been debated over the years as to who really wrote these rules. As the athletes developed, certain rules had to be changed. Teams would learn how to circumvent the rules for their benefit. Baseball wanted a balance between offense and defense and were flexible to change. When you think about it, certain rules have been maintained over the years. It is incredible how and why, or maybe it was a guess with the amount of distances that were established. How in the world did the rules makers, Cartwright, or someone else, ever come up with ninety feet between the bases or sixty feet six inches from the pitching rubber to home plate? These distances have stood forever. Only one can imagine if the base paths were ninety-five feet or the distance pitchers threw was sixty-five feet.

Some rules had to be added, changed, or tweaked for different reasons. There was an inordinate amount of collisions on the base paths. Some by accident and many were done on purpose. So baseball decided it had to take action, not only to make it fair, but the injuries were mounting up on the base paths. Obstruction was put into the rules, with the first version appearing in 1856. **1**

Just like "interference" is very rarely taught and gone over in youth baseball, so true it is for obstruction. Coaches and parents should not feel at all bad or inferior if they cannot grasp the difference of the two right away. I remember in the 2013 World Series between the Boston Red Sox and the St. Louis Cardinals, there was an obstruction situation that occurred and the announcer called it interference. Obstruction is the act of the fielder, while not in the act of fielding the ball impedes the baserunner from progressing on the base paths. Baserunners are allowed to run from base to base without being physically blocked by contact of the fielder. It is worth repeating from the previous chapter on interference that quite simply, interference is a "penalty" against the offense, and "obstruction" is a penalty against the defense. Here is an example of obstruction that I see year after year. Many times, as insinuated above, it is the coach who recognizes it and not the umpire. Suppose a batter hits the ball into left center field that looks like it could easily be a double, or even more. While the baserunner is rounding first base, he runs into the first baseman, who is standing in the base paths, and does not make an attempt to get out of the way. The collision of the two players will keep the baserunner from getting to second base. If this happens, the first baseman is called for "obstruction" and the baserunner is automatically given second base.

Coaches need to explain what "obstruction" is and should demonstrate at each infield position how to avoid it. Once I had the grasp of what obstruction is, I would practice it every year at the beginning of the season. We can't expect 10, 11 and 12 year-old kids to master both interference and obstruction. But if our job is to teach these players the great game of baseball, I think it is our obligation to expose them and explain what each of these calls is.

I have seen some youth coaches print out a one page explanation of the five most common controversial situation and rules in youth baseball and hand them out to the parents at the beginning of the season. I happen to think this is an excellent idea. If you have the time and the motivation, consider doing the same thing, and of course include interference and obstruction.

Remember, coaches and parents: the offense interferes, the defense obstructs.

1. Peter E. Meltzer, So You Think You Know Baseball?: A Fan's Guide to the Official Rules § 12.2 (2013)

**Related Resources:**

44 Baseball Mistakes & Corrections

Baseball Coaching: A Guide for the Youth Coach & Parent

Baserunning & Bunting Drills

*Chapter 9*

# Mistake #8
## Outfielders Throwing Mistakes

I remember when I played college football. Our coach used to press upon us that with eleven players on the offense, if ten do there assignments perfectly and only one player screws up, the play can still be a disaster. Sure enough, I saw this happen time and again. I now understand to a point what these big time coaches go through. How many times have we seen in basketball a player rebound and score the winning basket just because a player did not box out his man? Or in hockey, a player misses an open net goal because he was too anxious and he shot wide. Back to football. How many times have we seen a team drive down the field on a great drive and then on first and goal from the one yard line, an offensive player goes offsides and now they must score from the six-yard line and end up with a field goal instead of a sure seven points? On the youth level, it can even be more frustrating no matter what sport you are coaching. I can state it a million times, but we have to show patience and remember that we are coaching 10, 11 and 12-year-old kids.

In youth baseball it is no secret that the team that makes the least number of mistakes will usually end up on top in most of the games. If there are any mistakes that will drive a coach or parent crazy it is some of the mistakes you see that happen in the outfield. When there are mistakes in the infield, usually it can cost a team just an extra base, but a mistake in the outfield will usually be extra bases. A number of years ago we were playing a regular season game and a ball was hit into left field down the line for a hit. Now, I always teach my players to get the ball back to the pitcher so when he is on the rubber, the play is virtually halted. Apparently, some of the wonderful parents on my team took heed to what I was saying. So, in this game when the ball reached the left fielder, who retrieved it pretty deep, the parent of the player was screaming to throw the ball back to the pitcher. My third baseman and shortstop both had their hands up looking for the relay throw but the left fielder decided to throw the ball to the pitcher himself. It ended up being the perfect storm. The ball went sailing over the pitcher's head and from the angle it was thrown, went down past the first baseman almost all the way down the line. My right fielder was sleeping and the term "Little League Home Run" fit perfectly on this play as the baserunner rounded all the bases and went home.

A challenge for youth baseball coaches
has always been the player's parents, shouting instructions to their son or daughter. I have even seen some grandparents who came to watch the game get involved yelling instructions to their outfielder grandchild. I always go over this at the "parents meeting." The three most popular times when parents are yelling instructions are when their child is in the batter's box, when they are pitching, and when the baseball is hit to them. Going over this is important and it gives you the right to challenge the parent when they do yell instructions by reminding them what we went over at the beginning of the season. I have been successful with most parents and unsuccessful with a few. One thing I do know is that if you don't go over this, parents will feel they can and say anything from the stands. The best thing to do is practice. During your games keep you team aware when they will

have to throw to the lead base or home. In general, keeping the throwing distance short will help keep the mistakes down.

Of course, there are numerous mistakes that can happen in the outfield. The concept of getting the baseball to the pitcher is excellent to stop play, but carrying it out is another story. In youth baseball, the longer the throw the better the chance of a mistake. Teaching the concept of shorter rather than longer throws will save your teams runs and games. A quick drill reinforcing this concept is to have lines with three players in each line. On the go command the first person picks up the baseball, throws it to the player in the middle, who turns to his glove side and throws it to the last person in line. The first line done gets a point, then rotate the line. This simple drill will get your team used to the short throws. Turning to the glove side is the right technique to carry it through.

Teaching through drills is the best way to get a point across to your team. Telling them and then showing them the potential negative result of throwing a long ball to the pitcher will work well. Don't just tell your team, show them!

**Related Resources:**

44 Baseball Mistakes & Corrections

Baseball Coaching: A Guide for the Youth Coach & Parent

Fielding Drills & Techniques

Infield Team Play & Strategies

Baseball Chronicles 2: Article On Youth Coaching

*Chapter 10*

# Mistake #9
## Outfielders Holding Ball Too Long

When I was coach in the younger divisions, I would try to observe as many games in our league's major division as I could. I wanted to learn from other coaches the best way to do things, from how they placed their fielders to their dugout demeanor. I was adamant about becoming a good coach once I reached that division. In this particular game, I was watching, a lot of runs being scored. Toward the end of the game one team had runners on first and second. The batter hit the ball to right field. I could tell the way the outfielder charged the baseball that he was not the best player on the team. He did come up with the ball, and just before he did, the yelling began. I heard someone from the stands yell out to throw it home. But another parent who was louder was shouting for the fielder to throw the ball to third. Then I heard the coach yelling to throw it to second, meaning the second baseman. All this, plus some of the infielders were yelling for the ball. Meanwhile, at least two to three seconds passed with the outfield beginning and stopping his throw to three different locations. When he finally threw the ball to second, it was too late and both runners on base scored. On top of that, the fielder coming in from right field was visibly upset, and probably the dugout was the last place he wanted to be.

I've seen it happen in almost all sports, even at the professional level. In hockey I've seen players holding the puck too long when they should either shoot at the net or pass the puck to another teammate. This happens a lot on power plays, especially if the team has that rare two-man advantage. In basketball we see some point guards holding the ball too long when they should be trying to either penetrate the key or pass it off. Of course this will vary on each and every play. But, when it is your team that needs a basket, it can drive you crazy as a fan or a coach when the ball is held too long. There was a guard back in my day, Oscar Robertson, who seemed to know exactly how long to hold the basketball on each and every play. In football I've seen quarterbacks holding the ball way too long when they should run for a few yards or should be throwing the ball out of bounds. In baseball, the best defensive outfielders always were able to think ahead at lightening speed as to what to do with the ball when it was hit to them with men on base. Whether it was Willie Mays, Roberto Clemente, or Ken Griffey Jr., they all seemed to throw the ball, and never held it for an instant longer than they had to.

In youth sports though holding the ball is magnified even more so. Nothing frustrated me more in my 25 years coaching youth baseball than when there was a base hit and one of my outfielders would hold and hold and hold the ball with players on the bases. I've spoken about the vocal competition from the stands with parents yelling where to throw the ball. This is a major issue, and sometimes is the root of a player being undecided with the ball. When more than one fielder is demanding the ball at the same time, doubt comes into the mind of the outfielder.

I always teach my outfielders to get the ball back to the infield as soon as they can. I'm going it give you the best teaching advice you well ever have to resolve having an outfielder in youth baseball standing and just holding onto the baseball. Tell your players that when they are in the outfield and not sure what to do with the baseball, throw it to the person closest to them in the infield with the same color uniform. There you go! The player will at least begin to get the ball back to where the action is happening.

We practice situations. I have a drill called the "distraction drill." In this drill I set it up with players on base. I hit the ball to the outfielder with runners on base. I want to teach the outfielders where to throw the baseball. I instruct all my infielders to demand the ball and both my assistant coaches are yelling where to throw it. The fielder has to decide quickly the best course of action to make the proper throw. After the play I will discuss their decision. During games when there are players on base, I will yell out to certain fielders before the ball is pitched something like:

"Rob, if the ball is hit to you get the ball back in quickly to Eddie to keep the lead runner from going to third."

I have found that the more vocal a coach can be and not in an overbearing or obnoxious manner, the better chance his players will recognize his voice rather than the parents in the stands. As coaches we can tell our players what to do, but if we show them what to do, it will be conditioned into the minds of these young players better. Practicing is the best method for reinforcement in games as the season goes on to teach young players the importance of not holding the ball too long in the outfield with runners on base.

**Related Resources:**

44 Baseball Mistakes & Corrections

Baseball Coaching: A Guide for the Youth Coach & Parent

Baserunning & Bunting Drills

The 59 Minute Baseball Practice

Baseball Chronicles: Articles On Youth Coaching

*Chapter 11*

# Mistake #10
## Outfielders Not Charging Ball

There we were, in our league's minor division championship playoff series. We were winning by two runs going into the last inning. The opposing team got two quick runners on base. We then got two quick outs on strike outs after I changed pitchers. The next batter got two strikes on him and of course I was doing what most coaches do in this situation. I was anticipating getting another strike out, running out to congratulate the pitcher, and go up one game to none in the playoffs. But on the next pitch, the batter hit a seeing eye grounder between first and second. The ball was hit at medium speed and my right fielder was right in line to get the ball. But instead of charging the baseball and getting it back to the infield, he stood there waiting for the ball to get to him. He didn't charge the ball, which cost us the game. It seemed like minutes before the ball got to him. Meanwhile, not only did both runs score, but the person who hit the ball stretched a single into a double and ended up scoring one batter later with the winning run. Why my right fielder didn't charge the ball I don't know. But, we never really practiced or discussed the skill of charging the baseball.

Believe it or not, during the course of a youth baseball season some of the instruction you will give may be about landscaping. In fact, if you are a coach who is detailed orientated you'll become an amateur in landscaping yourself. I'll explain more a little later on.

In major league baseball I am always amazed by the play I see the third baseman make on a slow grounder as he charges the baseball. When he approaches it, he picks it up bare handed while moving and then throwing the ball to first base. It is an amazing play and beautiful to watch. The defensive player's concentration is incredible and he is focused 100% with incredible "eye-hand" coordination. In youth baseball, it is a different story completely on grounders. Players should be charging to pick up. I can only speculate, and there are no stats, but I'm convinced in youth baseball there are more errors in the outfield on ground balls then on fly balls. We all know that when errors and mistakes happen in the outfield it is usually more costly than if it happened in the infield. If a batter gets a line drive base hit, if the outfielder doesn't get in front of it then it gets by him. The batter can have an extra base hit. On the flip side, if the player does not charge the baseball correctly, the batter will also get extra bases.

There are different ways of teaching players in the outfield to field a ball on the ground coming to them. I prefer to keep it as simple as possible. When a player charges the baseball, he must keep his head down and watch the ball go into the glove. The baseball will be slowing down as it reaches the outfielder. This is simple physics as the ball rolls on the grass, it will lose speed because of the natural resistance from the surface. Of course, if the ball was bouncing to the player on concrete, it will also lose speed, but not as fast. You can explain this to your team in basic terms that your young players will understand. I have, and it usually sinks in with a lot of players.

A basic drill is to line your team up in left field. The coach takes a position between second and third base with a bucket of baseballs. You can either hit the baseball or just throw it hard on the ground to the first person in line. He must charge the baseball and watch it go into his glove. You want to emphasize fielding the baseball between the legs and not to be too upright. Advice I have for almost all basic drills is not to combine skills. If you are teaching your players how to charge a baseball, just stop at having the player catch it. Don't worry about him coming up to throw the baseball. After he catches the baseball have him toss the ball to the side underhanded. This way he is 100% focused on the skill you are trying to teach. I also have colored baseballs. The player has to yell out the color as the ball enters his glove, this way it forces him to keep his head down and follow the ball into the glove. With this basic drill, you can divide the team in half, using right field with another coach hitting between first and second. After the player charges the baseball, he goes to the end of the other line.

As far as the landscaping angle, you as coach have to know if the grass around the field has been cut recently or is wet. It is up to you to point this out to your team at the beginning and during the game. This is where your landscaping education will come in handy. It pays before each game to go out into the outfield and hit a grounder to one of your players just so you can determine how fast or slow the outfield grass is that day. Also remember, if your league plays on multiple fields that baseballs will not bounce the same on different fields.

**Related Resources:**

44 Baseball Mistakes & Corrections

Baseball Coaching: A Guide for the Youth Coach & Parent

Fielding Drills & Techniques

Infield Team Play & Strategies

Baseball Chronicles 2: Article On Youth Coaching

*Chapter 12*

# Mistake #11
## Backing Up The Wrong Way

Nothing exemplifies teamwork like the concept of backing up. Backing up your fellow players will save runs and win games over the course of a season. And it can win championships! If you follow major league baseball you probably either witnessed or heard about the 2001 playoffs between the New York Yankees and the Oakland A's where Derek Jeter backed up a play on the first base line. There were two outs in the bottom of the seventh inning. The Yankees were beating the A's 1-0. With a player running all the way from first base to home on a ball hit sharply down the right field line, the relay throw soared over the head of the relay man. Derek Jeter placed himself right in line with the ball as a backup at the first base line. On the overthrow, in one instance Jeter caught the baseball and tossed it to the catcher with a back hand flip and got the baserunner out. It was an incredible back up play by Jeter that helped turn that playoff series around. This player had the anticipation that a bad throw might happen and his back up effort was stunning. It was one of the greatest back up plays you will ever see in baseball.

In youth baseball it is obvious to all that backing up will not only save runs, but will save games, and in some cases seasons. I remember when I was coaching my son's minor league team in a tight game, we had a very sharp player at shortstop who had an incredible baseball I.Q. for a 10 year-old. I had a weak player at third base. There were runners on first and second. The other team had their best player up and I situated my shortstop to play deep in the hole toward second. On the next pitch there was a grounder to my third baseman. What happens many times in youth baseball happened here. The ball went through his legs. I kept my eye on the baserunner going to third and was ready to yell to my left fielder to throw the ball home. The next thing I saw was incredible, as my shortstop (all 90lbs. of him) had hustled his was toward third and scooped up the missed grounder and ran to the third base to step on it and get the force play. Plays like that are tattooed in my mind. It was pure instinct, and one of the best defensive plays I ever witnessed in all my years coaching. This player put himself in the perfect back-up position to get the out. And for the record, I had zero to do with the play. It was all my player doing it on his own. Most players in recreational youth baseball will not have the instinct or athletic ability as described above. I'm going to give you a couple of examples out of many of backing up what I consider the correct way.

First, on a steal of second base, it is imperative that the center fielder run towards the infield to back up, but not too close. If the player is backing up too close and the ball gets by the first back-up, it can get by the center fielder. His vision of the play will be handicapped because the other infielder not receiving the throw will be the first back up, which makes it all the more important not to get too close to the first back up. You have to go over this play and use different players at centerfield. Also, it is very important to reinforce to your players that outfield backups usually don't have to catch the ball cleanly but must get their body in from of it and stop or block the ball.

The second back up would be a steal of third base. I always instruct my left fielder when he sees the runner on second take off (he can only steal in our league when the ball crosses home) for third he must run directly in a straight line to the foul line. It is important he doesn't run at an angle, and then square shoulder himself toward home in the ready position. Here it is just as important that the left fielder does not get too close to third base. He needs room on a wild throw to stop or block the ball. By blocking the ball the player cannot let it get behind him. Keeping the ball in front of the player as a back-up is just as effective as catching it.

Back-ups in baseball will win championships but they must be done correctly and practiced correctly. There a lot of situations that require back-ups with players on base. Don't try to teach your players too much at one time. Feed them the different back-up situations as the season goes on and always reinforce them during the games and season. Move your players around and have each one experience bad throw and how we back up each other.

**Related Resources:**

44 Baseball Mistakes & Corrections

Baseball Coaching: A Guide for the Youth Coach & Parent

Fielding Drills & Techniques

Infield Team Play & Strategies

Winning Baseball Strategies

Baseball Chronicles: Articles On Youth Coaching

*Chapter 13*

# Mistake #12
## Infielders Reaching For The Baseball

When I watch NFL games on Sunday, I follow the wide receivers more closely than I do any other position on the field. I am amazed at some of the bad habits that these great athletes have and cannot seem to overcome. One of the bad habits I see by some is that they refuse to extend their arms to their maximum length and try to catch almost every pass against their body. They'll even jump when they don't have to just so they don't have to extend their arms. The receivers that cannot overcome this will usually be out of the league in a matter of time.

In youth baseball, most of the kids I see have an endless amount of energy. There are times that they seem to be going and going. So it is unbelievable to me that at times these same kids will stand like a statue with certain skills when they have to move their feet. We see this in basketball all the time on defense when players will stop moving their feet and just reach out for the ball while the offensive player will drive down the lane and shoot a lay up or pass it off for a sure basket. Imagine if a world class soccer goalie who is stationed in an 8 foot high by 24 foot long net just reaches for the soccer ball on saves rather than make a concerted effort to move their feet. Wouldn't the player look ridiculous?

In youth baseball, on ground balls to either side of the player, instead of moving their feet quickly to get in front of the ball, many times the player stands in one spot and reaches out for the ball. This is kind of the easy lazy way out. Part of our job as coaches is to get our fielders, especially our infielders, to move their feet to the baseball. I have a few basic drills for this that I'll share with you. I just want to emphasize to coaches and parents to start your kids at a young age getting them used to moving their feet in the direction of the ball.

The first drill is the "Goalie Drill." Place two cones about 8-10 feet apart. There is one player who is stationed between each cone. On the "go" command the coach, with a bucket of soft covered hard balls or even tennis balls, will try to continuously bounce the balls underhand past the player. The player, acting like a soccer or hockey goalie, will swat the ball away. It must be emphasized in this drill that the player need not control or catch the balls. He must just keep them from getting by him.

The second drill was one of my own kid's favorite drills that we did in the backyard for hours on end. We called it the "Dive Drill." I touched upon this drill previously, but it was so successful with my kids that I felt important to include it in this section. This drill is more of a backyard drill with a parent and their child rather than a team drill. Find a good patch of thick grass in your backyard or in the outfield at your school. Again, either using soft covered balls or tennis balls, begin to toss them to your child's left, then right, and keep mixing them up. Your child must move his feet quickly toward the ball and dive on the grass to stop it either with his glove or his body. I remember doing this drill when both my sons were around 9 years-old. Use your own discretion and keep this drill short. The kids will expend a tremendous amount of energy diving and getting up quickly. It is important in this drill that kids understand they can just swat the ball away and they don't necessarily have to catch the baseball.

A variation of the above "goalie drill' is the "turn around drill." In this drill the player has his back to a coach facing a fence or wall. The coach will throw or roll a ground ball to the player's left or right. When the ball is on it's way, the coach will yell out "Turn" and the player will turn around, see the ball, move toward it, and again swat at it before it reaches the fence. In this drill, we are combining a kind of reaction drill with teaching the players to move toward the ball. Coaches can alter the speed of the ball and the distance where they throw it from. Remember that kids love competition and this is a great drill to divide into teams and keep score.

Drills that kids love will be requested by them over the course of the season. This is one of the drills your team will request.

You can make up numerous drills so your players get used to moving their feet. The more different drills you have the more muscle memory is ingrained into your players. Telling them and reinforcing it during practices and the course of the game will make them better defensive players.

**Related Resources:**

Fielding Drills & Techniques

Infield Team Play & Strategies

The 59 Minute Baseball Practice

Baseball Chronicles: Articles On Youth Coaching

Baserunning & Bunting Drills

*Chapter 14*

# Mistake #13

## Infielders Toss Overhand On Short Throws

When you see a great point guard in basketball it is a beautiful thing to watch. On a fast break, most have excellent peripheral vision and can see the whole court. On most plays they know exactly when to pass the ball off, giving their team the best percentage of making a basket. Great point guards know what type of pass to make so the receiver of the ball can control it. They know when to whip a fast pass or an alley-oop or a touch pass that cannot be too fast. In most team sports at the professional level it is the same thing. Great quarterbacks know when to throw a bullet pass or a touch pass just as great passers in hockey are experts at knowing how fast to pass the puck to lead an open man. In youth sports, baseball in particular, some youth players have a hard time distinguishing how fast to throw the ball to a base to get an out. In their minds they try to react quickly to get the ball out of their glove and throw it to the base as hard as they can. If you are coach or a parent and observed youth baseball games you probably witnessed more than once infielders throwing the ball too hard on very short throws when, if they take their time and adjust their throw, it will be a sure out. This is a mistake I see year in and year out. As coaches we want our players to make the highest percentage play they can.

Here is the scenario. The batter hits a grounder to the second baseman's left side. His momentum has him moving toward first base. He fields the ball cleanly and as he comes up with the baseball ready to make the throw he is no more than 8-10 feet from the first baseman. Instead of throwing a catchable baseball, he throws it overhand at a speed that is almost impossible for the fielder to catch. The ball goes past the first baseman and instead of getting a sure out, the batter is now standing at second base in scoring position.

Coaches have to practice with their team to toss the ball underhand when they are right on top of the fielder covering the base. When the fielder throws the ball overhand, he has a hard time letting up on the ball in close distances. As I have said many times before, you can tell your players to toss it underhand if they are close to the base, or you can practice it so they at least get a feel for how to do it.

Here is a drill I set up to teach this, and in fact, two concepts are being taught. I always encourage cross sports drills. If you see a drill in another sport that might work for the sport you are coaching, then use it. For the underhand toss, I start with a drill at second base using a football. The concept of leading the fielder is also taught. I set up two lines, one at shortstop and one at second base. I stand behind the pitcher's mound and toss a football underhand to the shortstop. Only when he catches the ball can the second baseman break to second. The shortstop then leads the player, tossing the football underhand to the base. I do this for a while, then move on to baseballs. This drill works well. You can also move this drill to second, throwing tossing the ball to first base.

When teaching young players to toss the baseball underhand, some may have a tendency to toss it too high, which will drive coaches crazy. You have to point this out to your team and show them the right way and the wrong way to toss the baseball. The underhand technique should be practiced a few times during the season.

Here is a bonus on the underhand toss. When the bases are loaded with two outs, I teach my pitchers to toss the ball underhand to the catcher on a slow grounder that they field in front of the mound if their momentum is going toward home plate. I maintain this is the highest percentage for an out with the shortest distance to throw. Explain, then show your kids how when a pitcher's momentum is going forward, it is harder to stop, plant your foot, turn to first base, and throw it there. Remember what I said before that the shorter the throws the better chance of making less mistakes. The longer the throws, the better chance of mistakes happening.

When your pitcher is one of your better athletes, many times he can run home and beat the baserunner from third base, which is even a higher percentage play. Again you must practice this situation with your pitchers.

**Related Resources:**

44 Baseball Mistakes & Corrections

Baseball Coaching: A Guide for the Youth Coach & Parent

Fielding Drills & Techniques

Infield Team Play & Strategies

*Chapter 15*

# Mistake #14
## Second Baseman Not Backing Up

When I do my youth baseball-coaching clinics around the country, I always end it with a question and answer session. I try to answer every question I can, and if I can't answer a technical question, let's say on a baseball skill, I will tell the audience that I'm not 100% qualified to answer that question. In many of the clinics, a parent or coach will ask this question:

"Coach, what is the biggest mistake you see new or experienced youth baseball coaches make when coaching kids?"

I always answer this the same way. I see most youth baseball coaches try to over coach and under teach the game of baseball. By this I mean that a lot of coaches who may know more about techniques than me try to teach too many things in too short a time, especially to kids twelve years-old and under. When coaching a youth baseball team, think of it like you are building a house. You put in the foundation first and in the course of three or four months you frame it out and finish it up. Coaches are giving youth players too many things to digest at once. This is why you must practice and teach concepts weekly to reinforce them as the season goes on.

On back-ups, here is a technique that I put into play with my team because I learned the hard way when I began coaching. With runners on second and third or the bases loaded, and there is a wild pitch or a pass ball, the catcher goes to retrieve the baseball as the pitcher runs to cover home. The catcher tosses the ball to the pitcher at home. The toss though is wild, and ends up somewhere around the pitcher's mound. Another run scores. This mistake has cost teams not just wins, but in some cases championships.

To defend multiple runs from scoring, coaches will have a couple of options.

As noted on an errant toss to the pitcher covering home, the ball usually ends up somewhere around the base of the pitcher's mound. I coach my team that the second baseman should come to the base of the mound on a wild pitch or passed

ball. He will be in the most appropriate position to field the ball and prevent another run from scoring.

We are constantly practicing this when we go over wild pitches and passed balls in practice. You must always reinforce this and remind the second baseman during the game to go to the base of the mound. Some coaches prefer to have their first baseman go to the base of the mound to back-up the throw. I don't think it makes too much of a difference as long as there is a back up.

I began to also do this with only a player on 3rd. I have two reasons for doing this. First, suppose the runner from 3rd base somehow misses home. On the bad throw to the pitcher covering home, the back-up would be in position to possibly get the out on a throw, or even by running in to tag the baserunner. The second reason is to get the fielder in the habit of backing up the throw. This is what we coaches strive for. Good habits that develop into fundamentals.

Some coaches teach back-ups according to their personnel and who is playing at what base. Whichever way you decide to back-up the throw is fine, as long as it is done. I remember one year coaching our minor division when my first baseman was far and away my best fielder. I always tried to put him in as many back-up positions as I could because he knew what to do with the baseball.

When you are teaching your team these back-ups it is imperative that you move players around. Some coaches make the mistake of gluing players to certain positions and keeping them there. Youth baseball season last a few months. Players will miss games. You will have to substitute other players in their position. Players will also miss games for any number of reasons. At worst, have players practice different back-up positions at practice. When you are in a game, and it is a blow out either way, move players to other positions to get familiar with that position. You must coach to the ability of your team. If you are coaching a recreational team it is much different from coaching a competitive travel team.

**Related Resources:**

Fielding Drills & Techniques

Infield Team Play & Strategies

The 59 Minute Baseball Practice

Catching Drills & Techniques

*Chapter 16*

# Mistake #15
## Too Many Throws On Rundowns

I look at rundowns in youth baseball differently from most other youth coaches. Too many times I have seen in games that I'm involved in, or when opposing coaches or games I am observing, instruct their team on a rundown that if they cannot get the out right away, then run the baserunner back to the base where he came from. This is the easy way out. I teach my team that rundowns are a gift from the baseball gods to get a relatively easy out. Welcome rundowns, and only be satisfied when you produce an out. The techniques I see taught in rundowns are not the way I like to teach my players, which may be why many coaches are just happy with the status quo, as long as the baserunner did not advance a base.

There are a few reasons why rundowns are not successful in youth baseball. First off when presented with a rundown a lot of teams are seeing it for the first time because they do not practice it. This is a game situation that has to be practiced with players rotating fielding positions, and as baserunners.

Teams will also think that because it is a rundown they have to begin throwing the ball to each other right away. This is just the opposite of the ways I teach my team.

Still another reason many teams are not successful defending rundowns is that they throw the ball too many times. Because the players don't practice rundowns, when they are involved in one it may be their first experience. Players are yelling for the ball, coaches are yelling out instructions. and even parents in the stands are playing "coach" and doing their part to confuse the situation.

Let me break down my philosophy when it comes to rundowns. A key phrase I began to use a number of years ago is "sprint mode." I tell my players this, and even demonstrate how when a baserunner is running full tilt, it is very hard for him to stop short and change directions. I teach my players that we want to get the baserunner in a sprint mode.

Youth players seem to get into the habit of too many unnecessary throws, especially when the baserunner is dilly-dallying sideways. Too many throws allows the baserunner to stop and easily change directions.

The most basic philosophy I tell my players is the ideal number of throws in a rundown is none. The perfect situation is if one of the fielders gets the baserunner into this sprint mode and is able to run him down and tag him for the out. This will happen sometimes, depending on the personnel. A good point here to remember is that your fielders, even though they are 10-12 years-old, know what they are going to do next. The baserunner has to guess.

The second best number of throws besides none is only one. If your team practices rundowns, and understands getting the baserunner in a sprint mode, most of the outs will come from rundowns with one throw. And when you think about it, and picture the situation, you can understand why. It is extremely hard, and most times impossible, for the baserunner in a sprint mode to stop and change directions successfully. Remember to convey to your players that it is never a sure out unless they are able to hold onto the baseball. I've seen too many times when a team defends a rundown perfectly only to have the fielder tag the runner and the ball come loose because of the momentum the runner creates. Teach your players to squeeze the baseball. The pocket is a better place then the webbing when tagging.

A drill I use is to use two base paths, between first and second and third and home. Have a player in the middle of two fielders with a ball, and on the "go" command, the fielders try to get the out. This is also excellent practice for the baserunners when they are in a rundown during a game. You can set up a competition, giving the baserunner two points for getting to the base and the fielders getting one point for getting the out. Using two basepaths allows you to use six players at a time. Make sure you rotate players and positions. Kids love competition and when you set up a quality drill they will learn from and combine it with fair competition, you have hit a home run.

Besides this drill, practice rundowns and make sure you teach the other players to back up the throws. It makes little sense when during a rundown your outfielders stay out there far from the infield. I usually have my outfielders come closer to the infield just in case a throw is errant. Whenever players are backing up, if they are too close to the action, the ball can, and will, go past them. When practicing rundowns with my team I like to tell a player to make an errant throw on purpose, just to see how the fielders handle the situation.

**Related Resources:**

44 Baseball Mistakes & Corrections

Baserunning & Bunting Drills

Baseball Coaching: A Guide for the Youth Coach & Parent

The 59 Minute Baseball Practice

*Chapter 17*

# Mistake #16
## Tagging Baserunner on Thigh

In sports we see some crazy things. This is one of the reasons you and I love it! I've seen my football team with a running back on a clear path to the end zone somehow have his own knee on a high step pop the ball loose out of his hands, and a sure seven points turned into none. I've seen my basketball team with a player ahead of everyone on a fast break go in for the winning points on a lay-up only to miss, and miss bad, and then lose the game. In baseball, I have seen dozens of times the baseball beat the baserunner to the base, only to have the fielder tag the runner the wrong way, and the runner ends up being safe. How frustrating it is when a team plays a ball hit into the gap perfectly with two on-the-money relay throws and the third baseman tags the runner on the thigh while the player's foot reaches the base safely? This may sound ridiculous, as described, but I see it happen each and every year.

One of the biggest mistakes I see in youth baseball is coaches not teaching their players how to tag a baserunner out correctly. I'm sure if you have been around a while, the above scenario is all too common when the fielder tags the player's thigh instead of the "first skin", as I call it, when a baserunner gets to a base. Coaches have to teach players that on a play that is not a force at a base the fielder must "tag the dirt" at the "first skin" of the runner. The term "tag the dirt" means to obviously getting the glove down at dirt level.

Teaching players to "tag the dirt" should get the baserunner out every time. If a throw beats a baserunner to the base, there is really no excuse not to get the baserunner out. Why then do players insist on watching the baserunner slide into the base and tag his thigh?

Like most things, this is not practiced and it should be by coaches. I've said a million times before, and will say it again, you can tell the players how to do something, but if you show them and practice it, this will make all the difference in the world.

One of the first things I do with my team to teach how to tag correctly is to take the team into the outfield with some throw down bases. I then have a player lie down a foot away from the base and have every player with the baseball in their glove take turns taking the position of the defensive player and putting their glove down in front of the player's foot. Remember, muscle memory will help. This way the players actually see the situation where the glove is down in front of the feet of the baserunner. This may sound really elementary, but it works if you show them.

There is a drill I made up using a kick ball. It is called the "Kick Ball Tag Drill" or "Tag The Ball." I set it up around third base with the fielder ready to receive a throw. I time it so one of the coaches will throw a relay to the third baseman. I then time it that either another coach or myself will roll a kick ball to third base, knowing the fielder has already caught the ball. The fielder will then put his glove down and tag the kick ball that is actually simulating a baserunner sliding because it is moving toward the base. It is important to teach your players that once the glove is down, they might have to slide it to the left or right so the baserunner slides into it. This is a real easy drill to set up and very effective for teaching the players how to tag the baserunner. Even the weakest players on your team will understand the concept when they see the kick ball rolling and the players tagging it with their glove.

You can go back into the outfield after every player has at least one chance at the moving kick ball. You can practice this live. Find a nice patch of tall grass and have your baserunner take off their shoes. Time it just like the kick ball tag drill so the ball is at the base first and the player has to tag the dirt to get the out. Remind the players to squeeze the baseball so the slide does not knock it out of the glove. And, you must remind the players to follow the foot in case the player's slide comes on one side or the other.

Using the term "tag the dirt" in practice will carry over into games. Always be vocal and remind your fielders that if there is a man on base and no force to: "catch the relay and tag the dirt if the baserunner gets to third base." Giving up easy outs in youth baseball is one of the things that will drive a coach crazy.

As mentioned in the beginning, it is heart wrenching to do everything right and not get the out. Of course this will happen in youth baseball, but it is our job as coaches to try covering all aspects of the game in a fun creative way. If you practice this drill, your team should always get the out when the baseball reaches the base before the baserunner.

**Related Resources:**

Infield Team Play & Strategies

44 Baseball Mistakes & Corrections

Baserunning & Bunting Drills

Baseball Coaching: A Guide for the Youth Coach & Parent

*Chapter 18*

# Mistake #17
## Not Practicing Baserunning

Timo Perez played for the New York Mets and committed one of the biggest baserunning mistakes that remains in Met fans memories. It was the 2000 World Series against the New York Yankees. In game one, Perez was on first base. Todd Zeile hit a long fly ball that everyone thought was going out of the ball park for a home run. Perez slowed down on the base paths instead of running 100%. The ball hit the top of the wall and stayed in play. Perez ended up being thrown out at home trying to score. The Yankees went on to win the game and the World Series. I watched every pitch of that series and will swear that play set the tone for that World Series. Baserunning will win you games and baserunning can lose you games.

Remembering back when I coached t-ball, I can't tell you how many times things went array, and as parents, you just have to stand there laughing, not at the kids but at the situation. In many instances, baserunning would be challenging for the coaches and the parents to direct which way the t-ball baserunners should run. Some players would hit the ball off the batting tee and automatically begin to run to third base instead of first base until being redirected. Some t-ball players would hit the ball and run directly to second base. Fast forward 6 or 7 years and we still see many baserunning mistakes that are totally unnecessary. I remember when one of my players was rounding third base. He was one of my fastest baserunners and he never slowed up, and in fact was going so fast that he went around me behind the 3rd base coaching box. Inevitably he was thrown out easily at home plate. I can't tell you how many times I see teams either run themselves out of a rally or game. And on the flip side, I see teams exploit their baserunning situation in a positive manner and win a close game.

During one of the best seasons I ever had coaching, we were so aggressive on the bases it was scary for other teams. At the end of the season I was going through my scorebook and saw that my team was thrown out twenty-two times at home plate. On the surface this sounds like stupid baserunning. But, if you watched our team over the course of the season you'd see that baserunning was our greatest strength and our aggressiveness won us a ton of games that year.

When I first got involved in youth baseball, I was an assistant coach in the third base dugout. The opposing team had a runner on second base with no one out. At the time I was new and tried to listen to the coaching on both sides and absorb everything I could. I remember hearing the third base coach yelling to his baserunner on second base:

"Johnny, there are no outs. On a ground ball hit to the right side, take off. If it is hit to the left side, bounce off the base and start to run when the fielder releases the ball, listen to me."

I remember thinking that this was excellent coaching. But, I also immediately thought that this is something youth teams should practice and not just be told how to do. When I became manager, I devised a drill we called the "Bounce Drill." We would do this drill at almost every practice for five or ten minutes. Over the course of my 25 years of coaching, if there was ever one baserunning drill where I saw a "return on our investment," the "Bounce Drill" was it. If I ever authored a "Ten Commandments" of coaching youth baseball, one of them would read:

"Coaches must practice baserunning 5-10 minutes at every practice."

As I described the previous example, one of the biggest mistakes youth coaches make when it comes to baserunning is that when the player reaches base, the coach will advise him what to do if the ball is hit to a certain area. And this is the first time that the player hears these instructions and has to absorb what to do. Whether it is practicing coaching signs or going from first to third on a hit, coaches must spend time in practice going over baserunning. I have said, and still maintain that if coaches would practice baserunning in their practices 5-10 minutes at each practice, they can score 1-2 extra runs each game in youth baseball.

I'm going to say something that I have no scientific proof of but I've seen it with my own teams. If you are a coach and practice and put baserunning drills in each practice, there is a residual affect. Even the youngest players seem to pay attention closer when on base during a game than if you didn't practice baserunning. Again, I have no proof but I have seen it with my own teams.

Another thing about baserunning I have found out over the years is that players who are your fastest will not necessarily be your best baserunners. The best baserunners are those that have a natural instinct. When you practice certain concepts, they master it and become stars on the base paths. One player I had one year was nine for nine being safe on delayed steals. This player had an uncanny ability to time the delayed steal perfectly. We practiced the delayed steal, and he mastered it very quickly. It was incredible!

So, if you coach at any level, don't make the mistake of not practicing baserunning. You will see fabulous results if you do practice. And just remember that if you are not practicing baserunnig, other coaches are!

**Related Resources:**

44 Baseball Mistakes & Corrections

Baserunning & Bunting Drills

Baseball Coaching: A Guide for the Youth Coach & Parent

*Chapter 19*

# Mistake #18

## Baserunners Stopping At First Base

I am not, and have never been, a car-racing fan. With that said, I always thought it quite amazing at how fast these drivers go, especially when they negotiate the curves. I remember the legendary sports announcer, Howard Cosell, stating that race car drivers may be the best athletes in the world because their lives are relying on precise reflexes within a fraction of a second. In a race like the Indianapolis 500, these cars are going at a rate of speed averaging over 200 miles per hour and in some cases hitting 240 MPH. Now, imagine if in addition to winning the race by being the first car, part of the race is the car having to stop short right at the finish line to be declared the winner. As ridiculous as this sounds, think about some youth baseball players, who are running to first base on a grounder. As they reach the base, they stop short. And when I say stop, I mean stop short like first base is some kind of wall. We have all seen this happen, especially in the younger leagues. We coaches and parents have to teach players at the youngest age that they must run through the base. And, I'm not talking about 2 or 3 steps through the base, but 8-15 running steps. In stating the previous mistake about coaches not practicing baserunning, this is one of the most crucial mistakes players make in youth baseball, not running through the base. And it does not take a lot for

coaches to teach young players the right way to run to first base.

The most basic drill to do is to line up your players at home plate. Place a cone that is visible about 10-15 feet past first base (I believe in T-Ball this cone should be there at all games). On the "go" command, have the first player in line simulate he has a bat in his hands. He takes his imaginary swing and then runs to first base. He touches the base and has to run through it to the cone that was placed beyond the base. I have my players then turn toward foul territory. I usually start the next person in line when the player before him is about halfway up the first base line. After they turn into foul territory, they jog back to home plate and get to the end of the line. I always have a second coach at first base, who is cheerleading the runner to "touch the base and run through it." As in all drills, you want to keep all the players moving at all times if possible.

I mentioned how I have my players turn into foul territory after they touch first base and run through it. I know many of you who know the rules (probably better than me) will say that it doesn't matter which way the player turns as long as he doesn't make an "attempt toward second base." This is true, but the reason I have my players turn to foul territory is to ensure there is no problem in the case we have a young inexperienced base umpire who might call the player out if he turns to fair territory and is tagged. This happens once a year in my league when we have an inexperienced young base umpire who calls the play wrong. I am taking away the possibility of my player being called out by an umpire who may not know the rules well.

The habit of having the player run through the base is a precursor for telling the runner what to do. The player and team learns to listen to the first base coach, who has to be very vocal. On a hard hit ground ball or line drive, I teach my players to listen to two things. One is, "touch the base and run through it" and the other is, "touch the base and head to second." With the second instructions, the player is then taught to listen to two other commands; "stop and come back". The other is, "go to second and slide." All these commands are repeated a few times, and loud. If you have a first base coach who is afraid to shout the commands, get another coach.

All these commands and options are good and aggressive baseball, but it all starts with teaching the players at a young age to run through the base. As basic as it seems, practicing it will ensure muscle memory to take over once the real play occurs. Nevertheless, it is again one of those things that has to be practiced instead of just being told. Coaches in the younger divisions should make this drill a regular part of practice. You want your players to get into the habit of running, and running hard. Too many players will also slow up, and teaching them to run through the base will help reinforce them to run hard.

**Related Resources:**

Baserunning & Bunting Drills

44 Baseball Mistakes & Corrections

Baseball Coaching: A Guide for the Youth Coach & Parent

The 59 Minute Baseball Practice

Baseball Chronicles 1: Articles on Youth Coaching

Baseball Chronicles 2: Articles on Youth coaching

*Chapter 20*

# Mistake #19
## Players Not Sliding

Sometimes one play will not only determine the outcome of a game, but will be the defining play that people will always remember in sports yore. Whether it is John Havlicek stealing an inbound pass in a basketball playoff game or a young Cassius Clay beating Sonny Liston with a "phantom punch", or maybe a Bob Beamon shattering the Olympic long jump record. People will remember the play or event for decades and it will be passed down to generations. It was in the 2001 playoffs. The Yankees were playing the Oakland A's. In the seventh inning Terrance Long of the A's hits a ball off pitcher Mike Mussina down the right-field line. Shane Spencer did a good job fielding the ball, but made a wild overthrow that went over both cutoff men. Derek Jeter appears almost out of nowhere on the first base line to field the baseball, and then "flips" it home to catcher Jorge Posada, who puts the tag on Jeremy Giambi. Giambi didn't slide and is called out. This play became known as the 'Flip Play." Many believe this play changed the momentum of the series. The Yankees went on to win and ended up going to the World Series. In my mind, when I watched this play, Giambi would not have been called out if he slid like he was suppose to.

A few years later I was in a playoff game. We were playing a better team, but we were in this game. I told my team we cannot make more mistakes than our opponent or we would not be in a position to succeed. We were losing 5-3 and the strength of my batting order was coming up in the fifth inning. We had first and second with no out. I kept reminding my player on second base that if I send him home on a hit to slide. The batter hit the next pitch between the center fielder and right fielder. As soon as it was hit, like any coach should not do, I already started thinking ahead. With the runner on second scoring I was already thinking about getting the runner at first to third. Maybe if the other team threw it to third, the batter would end up on second base and we'd have second and third with no out. The center fielder made a great play moving to his left, scooping the ball up, and throwing it home. Still, as my baserunner was coming to third base, I yelled, like I do in these situations, "touch the base and go home and SLIDE." The throw incredibly was a perfect strike and arrived at the same time as my baserunner did. But for whatever reason, my player did not slide and he was tagged out. If he slid he would have probably beat it. To make matters worse, the catcher came up throwing to third base, getting my runner going there from first. Again, if my player slid, the chaos at home would have almost assured my first base baserunner getting to third safely.

I cannot emphasize enough how important it is for players to slide almost all the time. It takes effort and courage but the baserunner's chances of being safe are increased tremendously by sliding. In the Oakland-Yankee playoff game, Jeremy Giambi would have been safe. One play can determine the out come of a game, a playoff, a World Series. I have stated it many times that we have to remember we are coaching 10,11 and 12 year-old kids, but we have to practice baserunning and sliding.

I always teach my players to slide on any force out, even if they are going to be called out by 20 feet. I want other teams knowing that we always slide. This will sometimes cause the fielder to drop the easiest ball just knowing a player is coming in and sliding...and sliding cleanly.

I tell my player when they are on base if they are not sure to slide, then slide. I don't get into the different types of slides, but over the course of the season I will show them different situations. I will even teach players during the season that when sliding into second base on a steal to slide to the outfield side of the base. The furthest part away from home plate.

I mentioned that the outfield grass is the best place to practice sliding. Here is a hint. When you know you are going to have a practice with sliding, let the parents know to give their son old pants. When you take your players to the outfield grass, wet it down lightly if you can and have your players take off their cleats. You will have an effective sliding practice. One mistake you should mention is that some kids will begin their slide too early. Have your two best baserunners demonstrate first and mark where they began their slide. You can place a cone where you want your players to begin their slide.

Sliding is excellent fundamental baseball. Learn the correct techniques, teach your players, then practice it. Good sliding will keep you in games and also win some for your team. One more thing. If I was coach of the A's that year, Jeremy Giambi would have slid on that play. I guarantee it!

**Related Resources:**

Baserunning & Bunting Drills

44 Baseball Mistakes & Corrections

Baseball Coaching: A Guide for the Youth Coach & Parent

The 59 Minute Baseball Practice

*Chapter 21*

# Mistake #20

## Calling Time Out

If you are as old as I am, you probably remember the University of Michigan basketball team in 1993. They were called the "Fab Five", made up of an incredible talented starting five. The year before they lost in the finals to Duke. So, this was the year the team was going to avenge that loss. They were playing a very tough North Carolina team in the finals. Chris Webber was the star for Michigan. Toward the end of the game Michigan was down by two points. Six foot ten, Chris Webber, was handling the basketball. He saw that he was going to be trapped by the aggressive North Carolina defense and called time out. The problem was Michigan did not have any time outs remaining. Michigan was given a technical foul and lost the finals two years in a row. Webber went on to have a stellar NBA career, making the All Star team five times, but he will always be remembered for a calling that time out in college.

Years later, I am attending my son's Middle School baseball game. They were a talented team with a very knowledgeable and creative coach. He taught his kids to keep the glove on the baserunner as he gets up from his slide whenever the opposing team steals a base and is safe. Sure enough, in one of the games, a player who stole second base begins to get up from his slide, calling time out toward the nearest umpire. The umpire, though in the vicinity of the play, turned his back while the player was getting up after calling time and brushing himself off. The time out was never acknowledged and the umpire turned around again seeing the baserunner off the base being tagged. He immediately called him out. The young baserunner argued vehemently that he called time out, which in fact he did. The umpire explained why he was out and went over to the coach to do the same. When you call time out in sports with a referee or umpire, it is not like calling time out in your backyard. The timeout must be acknowledged.

I've seen a similar thing happen with the batter in the batter's box. The batter was getting ready to swing when he called for time, simultaneously stepping out of the batter's box. The umpire for whatever reason does not acknowledge the "time out" and the pitcher, who was starting his wind up, throws the ball in. The umpire calls a strike and the batter again argues that he had called time out. Just as in the previous example, the umpire explained that he did not grant the time out and it is not automatic just because a player calls it.

Whether it is in a basketball game, baseball game, or any other sport, as fundamental as it sounds, coaches and players have to understand time out and how and when to call them. I spend a short time at the beginning of the season going over how to call time out during a baseball game and what pitfalls there may be if you do not do it correctly. It is one of those things that come up once in a while when the time out is called incorrectly and a baserunner gives up an easy out or a batter gives up an easy strike.

When I do sliding drills in practice, I also teach the best method for a player to call time out. If coaches practice this method, it will carry over into other time out situations, and the player will learn to have his time out acknowledged before he moves. I have an umpire at this practice dressed in his uniform to make it official. It could be a young umpire from the league, who will jump at the chance to help out a coach. I have the players one at a time individually slide into a base, either second or third. The umpire will run over to the action and call safe. The player is instructed to call time out while he is on the ground and not to move until the umpire grants the time out. The kicker is I instruct the umpire to go deaf every three or four players for a good 8-10 seconds, frustrating the baserunner, who is frozen on the ground. This umpire finally turns to the players and acknowledges the time out, and then the baserunner can get up. By having the umpire not do anything for a while is reinforcing to the player(s) to be disciplined and not move until the umpires both hears his plea for a time out and acknowledges it. This is a very effective drill that will carry over to other time out situations on the baseball field.

On the flip side, like the example given above at my son's middle school, I instruct my players in the field to keep their glove on a player after he slides until the umpire acknowledges his called time out. I have gotten two or three easy outs over the years doing this.

**Related Resources:**

44 Baseball Mistakes & Corrections

Baserunning & Bunting Drills

Baseball Coaching: A Guide for the Youth Coach & Parent

The 59 Minute Baseball Practice

Baseball Chronicles 1

*Chapter 22*

# Mistake #21
## Runner On Third Leading Off Base

In the 2016 World Series The Chicago Cubs finally won! In that seventh game there was a noticeable piece of aggressive baserunning. Albert Almora Jr. came in to pinch run after Kyle Schwarber led off with a single. Kris Bryant then hit a fly ball to right centerfield. Most baserunners would go halfway down the line and go back to first base. Almora was smart enough to follow the fly ball. He tagged up from first and went into second base safely. He ended up scoring the leading run. This was brilliant and aggressive baserunning during a very tense game.

I am a huge proponent of aggressive baserunning. During one of my most successful seasons I ever had, my team was thrown out at home plate something like 22 times. This is a record that you normally would not brag about, and on the surface looks like it may have been a lot of dumb coaching from the third base coaching box. As a proponent of aggressive baserunning, I always put some time aside to practice baserunning at each and every practice. When you practice baserunning and reinforce fundamental baserunning concepts you will get a residual effect that the players will pay more attention to everything happening on the field better than other teams. I can't explain why, but this has always been the case with my teams.

A number of years ago I was watching our league's 12-year old All Star game play a home game against a very formidable opponent. In fact, we were playing against the best league in the county and historically we were never able to beat them. Our team had some of the best talent I ever saw at that age, and for one of the few times, we had a chance to beat this county juggernaut. I was coaching my oldest son's 8-year old team that year, but I wanted to watch as many games as possible to learn from the other coaches. This was a tight game and the score was 1-1 in the bottom of the 5$^{th}$ inning. We were up and the first batter made out. The second batter, the team's fastest baserunner, hit a screaming line drive into the right-center gap and stretched it into triple on a close play. Our home crowd, which numbered in the hundreds, big for our league, was going crazy. It was set up perfectly for our team to get the lead run across home plate and a possible win. A coach can't ask for a better situation. The lead runner was on third base, with less than two outs in the bottom of the second to the last inning. With our number three hitter up, the coach had a lot of options, including having the batter bunt to get the runner across. The coach decided to let the batter hit away. On the second pitch, the batter hit a fly ball into the left center field gap. It looked like it was catchable, and it was. Everyone in the ballpark was looking at the ball, knowing we would get the run across on an easy tag up. But, while the coach was watching the fly ball, the baserunner, for some reason, took a lead from third, about ten feet off the base. The center fielder caught the ball. The coach, realizing what the baserunner did, yelled at him to get back to the base and tag up. By the time the baserunner got back to third base the ball had already been thrown by the center fielder to the shortstop. The baserunner tagged up, but because his momentum going back to the base had to change toward home plate, he never had a chance.

By the time he tagged up and was ten feet down the line, the ball was on its way to the catcher. The coach was able to hold up the baserunner, but the next batter struck out and we ended up losing in extra innings. It was a huge disappointment.

Since that day, I have witnessed baserunners leading off third base for no reason.

There is nothing positive for a baserunner to lead off third base on a ball hit to the outfield to see if it is caught or not. We all know that players on third base have a tendency to take a lead when the ball is hit instead of staying on the base. Remember that baseball is a game of inches but physical momentum in baserunning is incredibly important! A good technique is for the player to stay on the base and not even look at the flight of the ball. He should stare at home plate. This is tough for a young player to do, but if practiced and explained he will follow your instructions.

The coach will watch the play closely. When the outfielder catches the ball, he will yell a predetermined word, like either "catch" or "go" signaling the baserunner at third to run home. Remember, he must slide. With this technique, we are taking the responsibility off the player's shoulders. Like all other techniques, it is 100 times better to practice the technique than tell the player what to do. Since I began using practicing it and reinforcing it when a player is on third base, my team has very rarely not scored from third base on a tag-up.

**Related Resources:**

Baserunning & Bunting Drills

44 Baseball Mistakes & Corrections

Drills & Techniques for Catchers

Baseball Coaching: A Guide for the Youth Coach & Parent

The 59 Minute Baseball Practice

*Chapter 23*

# Mistake #22
## Catcher Throws From Knees

In 2016, a New York Yankee rookie catcher, Gary Sanchez went wild in the short time he was brought up to the big leagues. He was hitting home runs at an incredible pace. In only fifty-three games he hit twenty home runs, which are Ruthian numbers over the course of a full season. Watching this talented player, it was not his hitting that impressed me. On one play, while he was catching, the opponent had a baserunner on second base, and on the next pitch, Sanchez, for some reason, on his knees, caught the pitch and threw a perfect ball to second base to pick off the baserunner. The play was truly magnificent.

For whatever reason, I have always had an affinity with the catching position. Being a baseball fan my whole life, even as youngster, I found it hard to fathom that the catchers I followed in the late 1950's and 1960's at times would catch both games of a double header. Today the starting catcher will very rarely catch a day game after a night game. It is still one of the most challenging positions in sports. I speak to baseball scouts from time to time, both on the professional and the college level. I always ask them the same question: What are you looking for this year? The answer very rarely changes. The priority that most scouts seem to always be looking for are two things: Lefty pitchers and quality catchers. The coaches and managers of professional organizations and college teams seem to always be complaining about the lack of lefty pitchers and fundamentally sound catchers. As far as the lefty pitcher, it is simple. You are either born a lefty or not born a lefty. As far as catchers, many scouts tell me that a lot of young players just don't want to put in the work involved behind the plate day after day. Like in basketball, many young players would rather shoot than play defense or rebound. I always use this basketball example when kids come out to warm up. Usually these days they take a basketball and go beyond the three-point line and begin shooting. If you are involved in youth or school sports, have you ever seen a basketball player come out and want to work on his defense or rebounding? I never have.

At the beginning of each year I get all my catchers together and tell them what I expect from them. I give a 5-minute lecture of how being a catcher in baseball is not an easy job and requires constant work for the whole game. The first time I ever witnessed the delayed steal in youth baseball, I was enthralled watching it succeed. I then began to study how the delayed steal was done from beginning to end. In case you are not familiar, the delayed steal occurs with a runner or runners on base, and they try to get to the next base after a pitch on the catcher's throw back to the pitcher. I observed how this was done and spoke to as many coaches my "senior" I could speak to. One of the most common aspects of the delayed steal I learned was the catcher having some kind of flaw when throwing the ball back to the pitcher. To a man, every one of the most successful coaches I spoke to said the same thing; "Never have your catcher throw from their knees when there are runners on base." This is very sound advice but in the course of a game or a season, the catcher can tire and slip up sometimes and throw from his knees.

A good opposing coach will smell blood. When he sees the catcher do this, he will attempt the delayed steal. No athlete at any age can throw the ball harder from their knees than from a standing position. There are no 11 and 12 Gary Sanchez's. I instruct my catchers that when there are players on base, they must stand up after every pitch and throw a line drive back to the pitcher. There is no half way about this. I begin in practices, and during the game, I am constantly yelling instructions when players are on base. And I remind the catcher to stand up and throw the ball back to the pitcher after every pitch!

Years ago on my minors team, I had a player named Andy who loved to catch. After the game, his uniform was covered from head to toe with dirt. He loved playing the part of the catcher and was a great listener. He lacked natural talent, but his hustle was incredible. For the age group at the time he was an excellent player. When I explained how to throw the ball back standing up with players on base he did it perfectly. Sometimes you may be better off with a catcher of less talent who understands what is required of him.

One more thing about catchers. We baseball coaches are trying to develop baseball players when we should include developing leaders with 10, 11 and 12-year old kids. Part of the problem is that we tend (I'm including myself) to over coach and over lead. We have to show more confidence in these kids as leaders. Catchers are a natural to be leaders, let's use them that way!

**Related Resources:**

Drills & Techniques for Catchers

44 Baseball Mistakes & Corrections

Baseball Coaching: A Guide for the Youth Coach & Parent

The 59 Minute Baseball Practice

Infield Team Play & Strategies

Fielding Drills & Techniques

*Chapter 24*

# Mistake #23
## Catchers Turning Body

One year, I had the best pitcher in the league on my team. He was a natural athlete. We were short catchers so my assistant and I agreed to try this player, who never even put on catching equipment. We just knew he would be a success behind the plate because of his athletic ability. We were 100% wrong! He struggled on every pitch. In fact, he turned his head and body on almost every pitch, whether he caught it on a fly or it hit the dirt. Not only did he struggle with his body turning, he really did not work the position and looked completely different from when he pitched. The game was a struggle for him, but also for us coaches, who did not cultivate enough players to fill in as catchers.

I touched on my affinity for catchers last chapter. I've seen the best catcher in our league leave baseball for another sport when he went from 12 to 13 years-old. I've also seen another player that I removed from the catching position because I felt it wasn't his position go on to be All-Conference in high school and later play catcher in college. I also remember one time I had a terrific center fielder, and he would literally catch almost anything hit to the outfield. He would get an incredible jump on the ball and would even make plays in left field and right field. He came to me wanting to try pitching. I was reluctant to give him a shot at it. I felt I couldn't afford to lose him in the outfield. Needless to say, I didn't give him the opportunity to pitch. As it turns out I should have. He ended up pitching for the high school team and did very well. Sometimes you never know about players. I should have been more flexible trying these players in different positions, especially those that play the catching position. I did learn from the above experiences to be patient with players if they have a desire to do something like learn a position, or even switch-hit. I know when we coach, we put our team on the field to win every game. I would advise you to think beyond just coaching for a championship like I used to early in my coaching career. If a player wants to learn to switch hit, play catcher, or even a lefty playing shortstop, why stop him? We coaches too often get caught up in coaching for the short-term picture rather than looking at the long term. If the worst athlete on your team comes up to you and asks to pitch, find an inning or two during a 15 or 20 game season where he can live his desire. We can be fierce competitors and at the same time raise a kid's self esteem.

The first example I gave of my player turning his head on almost every pitch is more common than not for young catchers. It usually happens when the ball hits the dirt. It really is a kind of natural flinch that can be overcome with practice.

One of the first things I explain to my catchers is that the equipment they wear works optimally as long as they are square to the pitcher. The body is well protected as long as they face the pitcher. When the catcher flinches or turns his body, he is exposing the ribs, the sides of the legs, and the knees from being hit with the baseball. I once had a player, who when he turned or flinched, exposed an area above his knee. That is exactly where he got hit. He ended up with a huge bruise that could have been prevented if he kept his body square to the pitcher.

One of the ways to overcome this turning of the body and/or head is to bounce soft covered balls at the catcher when he is behind the plate or anywhere there is room.

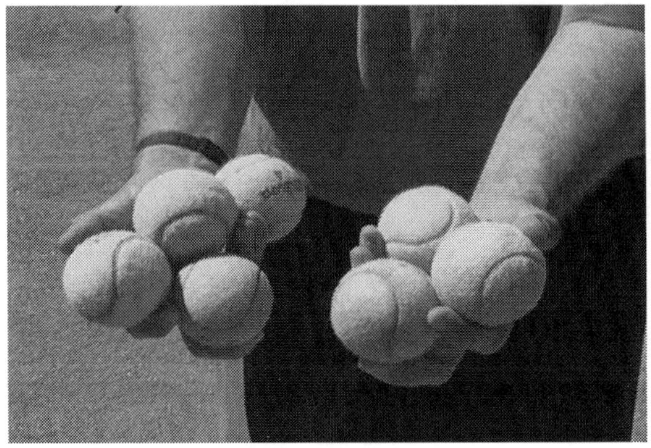

One of the best places for this drill is to use the fence along the sides of the field. The catcher must get down in his regular catching position. Instruct him that he must block the ball moving to his left or right or going down on his knees, but he cannot turn his head or body to the side. When I first start this drill, I do it very close to the catcher, only about five feet away from him. I then do this from about 15-20 feet away, and keep moving back. I start with tennis balls, then go to soft covered balls, and then to hard balls. With each progression of balls, I start close and move back. The muscle memory will condition the player to keep his body straight. This is one drill you don't want to rush through each repetition. After you throw the ball, give your catcher time to gather himself. Instruct him on how he did. You can also use Pickle Balls or Wiffle balls with this drill. Whatever ball will work is the ball to use, and progress from there. Doing this drill with your catchers a multiple times will overcome the turning of his body.

**Related Resources:**

Drills & Techniques for Catchers

44 Baseball Mistakes & Corrections

Baseball Coaching: A Guide for the Youth Coach & Parent

The 59 Minute Baseball Practice

Infield Team Play & Strategies

Fielding Drills & Techniques

*Chapter 25*

# Mistake #24
## Catcher Throws From Backstop

I got burned by my catcher, and in reality, by myself in one of the first minor games (8 & 9 years-old division) I ever coached. Coming from our Rookie division, I was excited because in this division teams were allowed to steal bases, bunt, and tag up. I was like a little kid in a candy store in my first game. I thought I had my team prepared, but I fooled myself. In the first inning, the other team got a man on second. There was a wild pitch. My catcher went to the screen to pick it up. He then threw it back to the pitcher from about fifteen feet behind home plate. To make matters worse, as soon as he let go of the baseball, he bent down to pick up his mask. The player on second went to third on the wild pitch and then came home on the long throw my catcher made back to the pitcher. This was a great lesson I learned!

I've always maintained that in youth baseball the team that makes the least amount of mistakes will win most games. Carrying this further, the team that throws the baseball around unnecessarily at long lengths and multiple times will lose more often than they will win. This is why in rundowns, as I have mentioned, the best number of throws is none and the second best is one throw. This is also why I teach my outfielders not to throw the ball directly back to the pitcher after getting possession of the baseball in the outfield. We have all heard the expression "Little League Home Run." For those of you who never heard it, think of a slow dribbler fielded by the pitcher. He overthrows the first baseman and the ball goes down the right field line. The right fielder rushes over to pick it up and overthrows the second baseman. The baserunner now is running to third base and the left fielder, who fielded the overthrow, picks it up and overthrows the third baseman. As the ball rolls to the screen, the baserunner goes home. There it is. A Little League home run! Things like this will happen. It is our job as baseball coaches to cut down the odds. We do so with a little tweaking, explanations, and a lot of practice.

After the above example of getting burned, I learned to turn the tables around to our advantage. We were playing a team, and I noticed that every time there was a passed ball or wild pitch, the catcher would field the ball and throw the ball back to the pitcher from wherever he picked up the baseball. He would be another 15-20 feet behind home plate. This was the same thing my catcher did in that first minor game I coached. I got my team together and told them when we get on base, not only are we taking a base on a passed ball, or wild pitch, but get ready for the long throw from the catcher and take another base on a delayed steal. We did it, and it worked. Finally, the coach instructed his catcher to throw the ball back to the pitcher when he was closer to home plate.

This is something I am adamant about with my catchers. I teach them: DO NOT THROW THE BALL FROM THE BACKSTOP TO THE PITCHER. During the game, I remind the catcher that if the ball gets by you, move up to home plate before you throw the ball back to the pitcher. I also tell my pitcher to remind the catcher during the game. Too many times the catcher will throw the ball to the pitcher, just about from the spot he picks up the ball up. The longer the distance from where the catcher picks the ball up and throws it to the pitcher, the more potential for a long and inaccurate throw.

I know by now you may be thinking, Coach Marty all these ideas are fundamentally sound, but there are not enough hours in the day to practice all this stuff. My answer is that I never try to give the players too much at once. I understand that with this age group and different talent, grasping all these ideas are tough. In the course of a 12-week season with say another 4 weeks of pre-season, go over only 2 or 3 of this mistakes I am addressing each week. Sure, you may get burned because one happened in a game and you hadn't gone over it yet. This is fine. Rome wasn't built in a day, and coaching young baseball players is a process that may encompass 3 or 4 years for what I am teaching. This is why I love getting a player when he is 9 or 10 and develop him over 3 or 4 years. There are so many aspects of youth baseball to go over and we coaches get caught up with trying to win the league championship instead of mastering the game's fundamentals and nuances that will make our kids better ball players. So remember, practice different concepts as the season goes on and reinforce them in games, but don't give your team too much to digest at one time.

**Related Resources:**

Drills & Techniques for Catchers

44 Baseball Mistakes & Corrections

Baseball Coaching: A Guide for the Youth Coach & Parent

The 59 Minute Baseball Practice

Infield Team Play & Strategies

Fielding Drills & Techniques

*Chapter 26*

# Mistake #25
## Not Including Pitchers In Fielding Drills

I never understood why when teams practice infield practice, there is almost always one large element that is missing. It is the pitcher. Unbeknownst to some coaches, the opposing team will hit baseballs to the pitching mound, in front of it, and to each side of it. It is not off limits in a game. They will also bunt, trying to make the pitcher field the ball.

If you follow major league baseball, think back or even look up the 2006 World Series. The Cardinals beat the Tigers four games to one. The thing that sticks in the minds of most baseball coaches is the huge number of errors the Tigers made. In particular, the Tiger pitchers and the errors they made. The Tigers had five straight games when there was at least one error by a pitcher. In fact, for those of you who love statistics, the Detroit Tigers made more errors in the 2006 World Series than the Cincinnati Red pitching staff did for the complete 2006 season. It is really incredible how the Tigers pitching staff looked like they never fielded a baseball. Another tidbit is that the whole Tiger team made eight errors and each of them were with men on base. How's that for timing? Contrast that fielding debacle with pitchers in the 1996 World Series. Andy Pettitte was in his second year with the New York Yankees. In game five of the Series, Pettitte was outstanding winning 1-0 against Atlanta Braves' John Smoltz. But, it was his fielding in the sixth inning that I will always remember. The first two batters got on base. The next batter bunted. It was an excellent bunt to the left side in front of home plate. Pettitte got off the mound like a cat, picked the ball up bare handed, and made a gutsy throw to third base to get the lead out on a force by inches. The next batter, Chipper Jones, hit a ball back to the mound that Pettitte fielded, threw to second, then on to first for an inning ending double play. He was phenomenal. In fact, there was no doubt in my mind that the Atlanta Braves were the more talented team of that World Series. We can see the contrast, and how important fielding can be by the pitcher.

Youth coaches spend lots of time doing fielding practice with both the infield and outfield. Overlooked is to include pitchers in their position on the pitcher's mound by giving them chances in the field. I believe the reason coaches overlook this is because usually the pitcher on the team is one of the better athletes. Coaches don't think it is necessary for them to practice fielding from the mound. They couldn't be more wrong. Situations with players on base and a ball hit back to the pitcher should be practiced. The different scenarios should be addressed, such as a runner at second with less than two outs. The pitcher can either hold the runner on base or look him back to second. Also, coaches should give all pitchers repetitions fielding bunts up each line.

Fielding situations should be practiced during the season that includes the pitcher. Here's a drill and simple strategy for your pitchers, and one that I have gone over before. The scenario is the bases are loaded with two outs. I've seen a slow dribbler hit to the pitcher, and instinctively or by instruction, the pitcher is taught with two-outs to get the final out at first base. Now think about it, the pitcher's momentum is going toward home plate. He must run to the baseball, stop, plant his feet, pick up the ball, and throw the ball to first base. A few years into my coaching career I thought it was much better if the pitcher flipped the ball home to the catcher with his foot on home plate to get the out. Think about it. The pitcher's momentum is going toward home plate. To me, it is a much safer option. In fact, with a slow runner at third, the pitcher shouldn't even flip the ball, but continue to home and step on the plate himself.

Most of the time, pitchers are focused only on pitching. I've seen their fielding responsibilities get away from them. This is overlooked and very under coached. It is good fundamentals to include your pitcher in these fielding drills. If a pitcher is to be a complete baseball player, he must be included in fielding drills. And in games the coach must reinforce reminding the pitcher what to do with the baseball if it is hit right back to him with runners on base.

**Related Resources:**

Pitching Drills & Techniques

44 Baseball Mistakes & Corrections

Baseball Coaching: A Guide for the Youth Coach & Parent

The 59 Minute Baseball Practice

Infield Team Play & Strategies

Fielding Drills & Techniques

*Chapter 27*

# Mistake #26

## Pitching When The Team Isn't Ready

Here is a situation that occurred when I was coaching our league's rookie division. My team was taking the field in the bottom of the first inning. I was talking to my coach in the dugout. We were both very inexperienced at the time. Our pitcher finished his warm ups. The first batter got up, and on the first pitch hit a fly ball to left field. The problem was my left fielder wasn't there! The ball dropped and my shortstop had to go to the outfield to field the baseball. I thought I had lost a player somewhere until I noticed him at the fence with his parents. They were giving him his water bottle along with some food. Even when my shortstop got the ball back, my left fielder and his parents were oblivious to what was going on. This was a huge lesson for me.

In sports, many times we see situations where a player is not expecting the ball or play to him, and all of a sudden he gets a surprise. In football, we have all seen it when a quarterback is in the shotgun formation and the center snaps the ball to him when he is not ready. Or how about a running back not expecting a hand-off. How about the Dan Marino fake spike years ago that caught the whole New York Jet defense by surprise. In basketball we've seen the savvy passing guard throw a no look pass to his forward, who was not expecting the ball, and a great opportunity for a basket is missed.

In youth baseball there are situations that occur when the ball is live and some of the fielding team is not ready to field the baseball. I was coaching my middle son's minor league baseball team. They were 9 year-olds. We had our best pitcher on the mound. This kid loved to pitch and he worked very quickly on the mound. It was something like the 4th or 5th inning as I remember it. On one pitch, the batter hit a foul ball behind first base in foul territory. The right fielder, first baseman, and second baseman all went after the ball unsuccessfully as it dropped in front of the fence. The next thing I know our pitcher pitched the next ball and the batter hit a routine ground ball toward second. The problem was my second baseman was still coming back from foul territory after trying to catch the previous hit ball. When the second baseman heard me yelling and saw what was happening he sprinted toward his position to try catching the ground ball. Too late. The ball dribbled through right where the he was suppose to be. There are a few things about this play. My pitcher should never have pitched the baseball. After this play, I began to teach all my pitchers to do the same thing. After every play, I tell my pitchers to stand off or behind the pitching rubber. They are to turn their back and look out into the field. I want them to scan the whole field. When they are sure the players are ready, only then can he pitch. Notice, I'm not saying they must be in the "ready position", but they must look ready. I have seen this happen more than once with other teams on a similar type of play. A ball is hit somewhere in the field and it is taking longer for the players in the vicinity of the play to get back to their positions. The pitcher not looking behind him will pitch without his team ready.

In this situation, I also want my players, who were near the play to hustle back to their positions. This also helps curtail a "not ready to field" situation. And last but not least, the coach or manger, meaning you, must be focused 100% on what is happening on the field. If you see the players are not ready, you must shout to your pitcher not to pitch until the team is ready. I've been in dugouts where the manager and coaches are discussing the baseball game that was on television the night before. This is unacceptable.

I want to mention here that as your read this book you will notice that I am always having the coach yell out things to their players. It is a constant matter of teaching and reinforcing over and over again. This is what coaching is all about. Not just hitting batting practice but teaching your players equally the big things as well as the small nuances. I learned years ago you can be a vocal coach and not be obnoxious or make a scene. It is a two edge blade when you are vocal reinforcing instructions. You are making your team better, ready to make a play in the field, or throw to the right base. You are also keeping yourself in the game at all times. This is what makes better players, better teams, and better winners!

**Related Resources:**

Winning Baseball Strategies

Pitching Drills & Techniques

44 Baseball Mistakes & Corrections

Baseball Coaching: A Guide for the Youth Coach & Parent

Infield Team Play & Strategies

*Chapter 28*

# Mistake #27

## Pitcher Fielding Mistakes

A number of years ago the New York Mets pitcher ran over to cover first base on a ball hit to the right side of the infield. The Mets were playing the Braves. David Cone got to first base with what looked to be in plenty of time. The umpire though called the runner safe. Cone went into a tirade. The problem was there were two other Braves on base at the time. While Cone was arguing, both runs scored. David Cone lost his focus after a wrong call. His arguing cost his team two easy runs.

Young players can be a sensitive bunch to teach. As coaches, we have to get it across to players, especially pitchers, that their responsibility doesn't end when the ball arrives at home plate from the pitcher's mound. Young players will many times forget the rest of their responsibility because they are focused so much on only throwing the baseball. This is why we have to remind them to cover home on wild pitch, back-up third base on a long hit, or cover first base on a ball hit to the right side of the infield. I saw a pitcher one time throw his glove down after a batter hit a long drive that hit the right center field fence. He stood there with his head down. The batter rounded the bases. There was going to be a close play at third base. The baserunner was safe because of an overthrow. Guess who should have been backing up? You guessed it, the pitcher. He was so disappointed about giving up the long hit that he lost his focus on his other responsibilities.

We touched on the fact that many coaches don't have their pitchers practice fielding. A number of years ago I was involved in a very tight playoff game. I believe at the time we were winning 2-1 and it was late in the game. When players are on base I always remind my infield by shouting out instructions such as, "Runner at second and there is one out. Hit to the right side, get the out at first. Hit to the left side, try to hold the runner before throwing the ball to first". I also try to remind the pitcher, but with less instructions. I'll tell him, "Shane, runner at second with one out".

In my experience it is best not to give too much instruction to the pitcher during the game. He is usually focused 100% on his pitching. Sometimes when you tell him something, he will be shaking his head like he understands you, but really hasn't heard a thing. It is quite normal. This is why it is so important to have pitchers practice situational fielding. They have to get use to being able to multitask on the field. Pitchers should pitch the ball the best they can and make the fielding play to stop any extra advance by the baserunner or runners. In the game situation I'm describing, there was a runner on second base with one out. I reminded my fielders and my pitcher of the situation. On the next pitch, the ball was hit sharply right to the pitcher. He immediately turned toward first base and made the throw for the out. He did not even acknowledge there was a runner at second, nor did he attempt to hold him from advancing to the next base, which the baserunner did. I could have screamed out at him to throw the ball to third base or check the

baserunner, but this would not have been a good move. My experience has been that when the ball is in play and a minor mistake is being made, if you yell instructions in the middle of a play, sometimes this will exacerbate the problem.

You can compound the mistakes by creating multiple mistakes. Many times the response will depend on the age and ability of the players if you yell instructions.

I teach all my players that when they are in the field and there are runners on base, to ask themselves "If the ball is hit to me, where should I throw it"? The pitcher should really do the same thing. When there are baserunners, I tell my pitchers that before they begin their wind-up to at least ask themselves if it is a force situation or not. I've seen it a number of times when the pitcher either doesn't throw the baseball or throws it to a lead base when there is no force. Many coaches disagree with me when I tell them at clinics that I try to yell out instructions. Please keep in mind that my instructions are limited, and very rarely yelled out when the ball is live.

I have found the best way to teach pitchers fielding skills it to practice different situations live. I would do this once a week or every other week depending on the learning curve of my pitchers. When you are practicing, mix it up a bit. Tell the baserunner to delay running, then to run even though he will be a sure out. There is nothing like experiencing practical situations.

**Related Resources:**

Pitching Drills & Techniques

44 Baseball Mistakes & Corrections

Baseball Coaching: A Guide for the Youth Coach & Parent

Infield Team Play & Strategies

Baseball Chronicles: A Guide for the Youth Coach

*Chapter 29*

# Mistake #28
## Rocker Step Too Long

Some basic fundamentals with regard to hitting and pitching come up year after year. I will never be mistaken for a major league pitching coach. With that said, I am confident enough to notice flaws with young pitchers and correct some . I see a number of my pitchers go on to pitch with success for their school team and beyond. I spent numerous years going to clinics and listening to pitching coaches at all levels. After some of these clinics, I have come away more confused than when I went in. I decided long ago that the best way to teach young players about pitching and hitting is to keep the instruction at a minimum. Remember, under coaching is much better than over coaching. Especially with young players. If you notice fifteen mistakes with a hitter or pitcher, I maintain you are much better off picking and choosing what you consider to be the five most important mistakes and correcting them. The reason is to keep it simple with young players. Sometimes when you correct five mistakes they somehow are related to the others and they will take care of themselves. Many times it is not as easy as it sounds. Many times your players will be taking pitching lessons, and when I would make a suggestion my player would say:

"Yea, but coach Marty, coach Larry, my pitching coach, told me not to do it the way you have been telling me to do it, but to do it this way instead."

And then I would hear it from the parents about how they are paying an ex-minor league pitcher $150.00 an hour and I don't know anything about pitching. I try to find out the players that are receiving pitching lessons and those that aren't. I try to respect the ones that are getting lessons. I learned in life there are some battles that you can never win. And this is one of them. With that said, I see repeatedly young pitchers begin their wind-up incorrectly, and thus the whole pitching motion from beginning to end is screwed up. In all sports the athlete must consistently master their skill in such a way, because if one part is slightly off, it will affect everything else. If you watch NBA basketball players shoot foul shots, the most successful ones do it the exact same way each and every time.

With pitchers in youth baseball, the rocker step, or the beginning step the pitcher takes, is of the most importance. Pitchers need to be balanced. There are two methods with the rocker step. One has the pitcher move his foot slightly behind the rubber then bring it forward and continue his wind-up. The second method is for the pitcher to step slightly to one side, then continue his wind-up. Many young pitchers are going with the second method, the step to the side. I happen to like the first method, with a small step behind the rubber then coming forward. My reasoning is that the player will be throwing it forward, so why not have him step forward (after he steps back) then make the pitch. The biggest mistake I see pitchers make with regards to the rocker step is that when they step back, they are stepping too far. The step back should not go past the heel of the stationary foot.

When the player steps too far back, his next action of going into the wind-up increases the possibility of becoming off-balance. So, a small step is better than a large one. About 6 inches should be fine. The weight should be on the ball or front of the rocker step foot. The part of the foot considered the ball is the portion of the between your arch and toes. Many coaches teach that the heel should not touch the ground. They say this causes improper weight transfer. The whole point of the rocker step is to develop rhythm, tempo, and momentum.

A problem I see in most leagues that I have addressed is that many pitching mounds are not manicured sufficiently. And many times there is a hole right in front of the rubber that causes the pitcher to become off-balance when stepping into it. On a given Saturday in the spring some fields have games starting at 9am and finishing at 11pm at night. Once the games start it is tough to keep the fields maintained as well as it was for the first game.

In summing up, the rocker step is an important part of pitching that even the most inexperienced coach can teach. When teaching the rocker step, have your pitcher concentrate on the step itself without worrying about throwing strikes. Throwing into an empty screen is an excellent technique, Lately I have seen coaches take film clips with their smart phone and show the clip to the pitcher. This is a great way to reinforce the rocker step and it's importance.

**Related Resources:**

Pitching Drills & Techniques

44 Baseball Mistakes & Corrections

Baseball Coaching: A Guide for the Youth Coach & Parent

The 59 Minute Baseball Practice

*Chapter 30*

# Mistake #29

## Pitcher's Elbow Drops

In baseball, injuries are becoming more and more common place, and at a younger age. Players are in multiple leagues and many do not follow pitch rules, which is a must. Overuse could be the number one reason youth baseball pitchers get injured.

It is impossible for every youth coach to keep track of every player on their team and what they are doing on other teams. As youth coaches, please be aware of the risk factors involved in pitching a baseball. I mentioned overuse, but age is a huge factor with kids still developing physically from ages 9-14, and injuries can be permanent. Throwing a curveball is a risk factor as well as improper pitching techniques. If you are going to coach for a few years, you owe it to yourself and your team to be knowledgeable of the most common injuries for youth pitchers. Even though you may not be an expert in pitching, there are certain things you can see that can be corrected. As a coach, you want to give the pitcher basic fundamentals. Don't feel intimidated or nervous when you hear the other coach(es) yell out things like:

"Rotate the hips quicker", or "Follow through on your heels, chin over stomach."

I coached youth baseball for 25 years, and this I can tell you, most coaches mean well, but they over coach and sometimes make things confusing for 10, 11 and 12 year-old kids. Do I wish I knew more about pitching and hitting techniques? Of course I do, but I also know the audience I am working with. Take the information I give you. Research others and develop your own theory for teaching technique. We want to put kids in the best position to succeed, whether it is pitching, batting, or in another sport like taking a free throw shot. One occurrence I see all the time are pitchers dropping their elbow below their shoulder. Unfortunately in today's youth baseball, pitchers are hurting their shoulders, elbows, and even their hips. When one analyzes the baseball pitch, it is not a natural motion for the human body. This is why baseball pitchers need recovery days after they pitch a game. In some youth baseball leagues if a pitcher throws 66 or more pitches, he is required to rest four calendar days before he can pitch in a game again. A good analogy is softball pitchers. The motion of the softball pitcher is more natural than the baseball pitcher. If you stand in front of the mirror and practice the underhand softball motion you will see and feel the natural underhand movement of the arm. This is why softball pitchers have been known to pitch double headers and in some national tournaments triple-headers. There is no pitch limit in softball that I know of. Stand in front the mirror again. Practice throwing like a major league pitcher. You can see and feel the movement of the arm is not as fluid or natural as it is pitching a softball underhand.

In baseball, when the youth pitcher's elbow drops, their hand is being forced to be closer to their own head. We want the elbow at or a little above shoulder height and the hand must be outside the elbow.

I'll try to be as simple as I can. When the elbow drops and the hand gets next to the head, the release point is not where it should be. You may have a top pitcher who has great form, but if he went to a pool party the same day he is pitching, his arm might be a little tired you may see his elbow drop. It can be hard to distinguish, but I have noticed, in general, when one of my pitchers is tired, he usually misses "high" and consistently falls behind the batter. On the high school level when the pitcher's elbow drops, the change in his velocity is very noticeable. If you speak to knowledgeable high school coaches they will tell you that when the elbow drops the arm will kind of lag and the pitcher's hip rotation will be stifled, hence adding to the diminished velocity.

Sometimes just making young players aware of a flaw is not good enough. I was at a clinic once and the pitching coach held a broom stick at the point in front of the mound where the pitcher should release the ball. Without holding a baseball and doing his pitching motion, the pitcher would keep his elbow at the height of the stick. I've done this and it is effective for some (not all) youth pitchers. Some coaches also like to have pitchers throw next to a fence or wall so when they pitch they must come over the top and this helps reinforce the elbow being at shoulder height.

**Related Resources:**

Pitching Drills & Techniques

44 Baseball Mistakes & Corrections

Baseball Coaching: A Guide for the Youth Coach & Parent

Infield Team Play & Strategies

Baseball Chronicles: A Guide for the Youth Coach

*Chapter 31*

# Mistake #30

## Full Wind Up Instead Of The Stretch

I had a pitcher, William, who would consistently throw strikes in practice. Once he got into a game he could not find home plate. It drove me crazy trying to figure out why. I then remembered the following story and adjusted him so he would pitch from the set position. He started throwing strikes!

I have been a lifelong New York Yankees baseball fan. I was fortunate to live about 35 minutes away from Yankee Stadium. As a youth in the early 1960's I was able to see a lot of Yankee legends we hear about every day: Mickey Mantle, Roger Maris, Yogi Berra, Whitey Ford, etc. After the organization went through a dry spell for a number of years, they bounced back into contention in the late 1970's. I was drawn to a pitcher named Ron Guidry. I liked the way he carried himself on the field. He got up to the majors at 25, not too young and really not too old. When he first came up to the majors, he was terrific, but he was not consistent and could be wild. The General Manager wanted to send Guidry back down to the minors, but the Yankee manager at the time, Billy Martin, saw Guidry's potential and fought to keep him in the Majors. Martin, with the blessing of his pitching coach, came up with the idea to have him pitch out of the stretch position on every pitch, whether there were 3 men on base or no one on base. This little adjustment changed Guidry as a pitcher, and the rest is history. Ron Guidry went on to become one of the better pitchers, not only for the New York Yankees, but in all of Major League Baseball. Guidry went on to win 170 games, was a four time All-Star, a Cy Young award winner, and he led the American League in wins and lowest ERA twice. Who knows where he would have been if Billy Martin didn't make this little adjustment of having him pitch from the stretch on every pitch. Once he got his control and throwing motion in tact, he began pitching from the full wind-up.

I am a great believer in having young pitchers learn to pitch from the stretch position if they are a little wild. For young pitchers 8-12 years-old, there is very little if any loss of velocity. But, remember at this young age, we are more concerned with the pitcher throwing strikes then velocity. Also, there is less that can go wrong when pitching out of the stretch. There are less moving parts and the mechanics are simplified to such a point that balance, for instance, is almost assured from the stretch position.

I truly believe that teaching a youth pitcher to pitch out of the stretch will help his accuracy in the long run. We are trying to build a foundation with mechanics and this technique will help. Keep in mind that if the pitcher goes on to pitch beyond 12 years-old, he will have to learn the stretch anyway to hold baserunners on. If you do have a pitcher who pitches lights out from the full wind-up, don't do a thing.

I would impose my own pitching schedule, depending on the pitcher. So for one pitcher I may have him throw from the stretch for say 3-5 games. If he is throwing strikes, I would then in practice have him throw with the full wind-up. Then I would mix it up, say two innings from the stretch and 3 or 4 using the full wind-up.

There is nothing set in stone, and you can also ask the pitcher what is he comfortable with doing. Word of caution. Just as I mentioned when talking about the rocker step, make sure when you play your games, the pitching mound is manicured correctly so your pitchers are comfortable out of the stretch or with the full wind-up. This has been a huge problem over the years that I have mentioned. With all the use a field gets during baseball season, the hole dug in front of the pitching rubber can become a hazard for pitchers trying to keep their balance in the full wind-up.

**Related Resources:**

Pitching Drills & Techniques

44 Baseball Mistakes & Corrections

Baseball Coaching: A Guide for the Youth Coach & Parent

The 59 Minute Baseball Practice

Infield Team Play & Strategies

Fielding Drills & Techniques

*Chapter 32*

# Mistake #31

## Pitchers Covering 1st Base On Grounder To Right Side of Infield

Because I am such a big fan of baseball, there are certain parts of the game I watch closely and appreciate. I love great fielding pitchers! I mentioned earlier how a pitcher fielding is one of the most neglected parts of youth baseball. Having a great fielding pitcher will save games for teams. In the previous article I mentioned the merits of Ron Guidry. His fielding was almost second to none when he pitched. He completed his wind up and follow through perfectly. Both shoulders always faced home plate evenly, putting him in a perfectly balanced fielding position. Greg Maddux, and going back further, Jim Kaat, were also two of the best fielding pitchers I ever saw. When you have great fielding pitchers, like the three mentioned, it is like having a tenth player on your team. The rest of the infielders more relaxed when they know they have a top fielder pitching.

Great fielding pitchers don't just mean getting off the mound quickly. It means having excellent awareness of the baserunners and where to throw the ball, as well as knowing when and where to back-up on the field. Great fielding pitchers are just not really common anymore. Youth coaches should work with their pitchers to excel at fielding.

In addition to what was just mentioned, fielding is just not limited to come-backers right to the pitcher's mound. It is a combination of learning how to become instinctive on plays, such as bunts. It is also a matter of getting over to the right side of the infield on ground balls to cover first or fielding a ball on the move and tossing to first for the out.

One of the biggest mistakes coaches make is not having pitchers practice how to field a ball hit to the right side of the infield-or to the pitcher's left side. It is one of those situations that the coach must remind the pitcher of the situation during the game, but coaches tend not to practice this. Too many times pitchers think their job begins and ends with throwing the ball to the catcher. And, one of the reasons is that pitchers are usually the best athletes on the team and they think their pitcher can make almost any play. Don't get caught up in assuming an important part of baseball should not be practiced because of talent. As a coach, one of your jobs is to set good precedents and lessons for your kids.

When a ball is hit on the ground or a line drive to the pitcher's left side, he must run along a designated path to cover first base. It is good to teach this process both on ground balls and line drives (a line drive in case it is knocked down). Many times the first baseman will be able to field the ball and make the play at first himself. This is where good communication comes into play. The first baseman must initiate "I got it" or "All Mine" loud and clear so the pitcher will yield to the first baseman to make the play by himself. Though this sounds very basic, unless you practice this there will be mayhem and collisions at first base. Just remember, this is youth baseball, and no matter how often you practice the pitcher covering first on a ground ball, there will still be collisions. The method being talked about and shown will put your players in the best position to succeed on the field.

When the pitcher runs to cover first base, he should not do it in a straight line. He should run toward the first base line 8-10 feet short of first and turn up the line, parallel to it. When executing this play, pitchers will cross the first base line opening up the chances for a collision at first base.

When the first baseman fields the baseball he must turn and toss the ball before the pitcher gets to first base. We want the pitcher to be able to look at both the baseball coming to him and the base to step on. He cannot do this at the same time. Do not get caught up in the most minute details of how and why we toss the ball to the pitcher covering first base a certain way. When you practice this play over the course of a season in practice, the pitcher and first baseman will figure things out for themselves. Point things out but do not overdue the instruction.

**Related Resources:**

Pitching Drills & Techniques

44 Baseball Mistakes & Corrections

Baseball Coaching: A Guide for the Youth Coach & Parent

The 59 Minute Baseball Practice

Infield Team Play & Strategies

Fielding Drills & Techniques

*Chapter 33*

# Mistake #32
## Watching The Lead Baserunner Back To The Rubber

In all sports, coaches and managers are always playing a chess game, trying to think one or two moves ahead and outsmart the opposing manager. When I coach a baseball team, I always try to keep my eyes focused 100% on the field. I'm looking for situations or tendencies I might catch the other team doing. It may be the pitcher when he throws or it may be a hitter in the batter's box. If you pay close attention on the field, you will catch at least one tendency during a game. I'll go even further. I've had players who play for me pick up tendencies by the opposition. Yes that's right! I have had 10, 11 and 12 year-old kids pick up things on the field before I notice them. This is one of the reasons why baseball is such a great game.

In the 2009 World Series, I witnessed what I believe to be one of the best baserunning plays. It was a combination of noticing a team's tendency and devising a pro-active plan of how to exploit that tendency. The Yankees were playing the Philadelphia Phillies in the 2009 World Series. Thirty-five year-old, Johnny Damon, was facing pitcher, Brad Lidge. Damon was batting and kept fouling balls off and finally hit a soft single into the outfield. The next batter was Mark Teixeira. Teixeira has the reputation for being a pull hitter when he bats lefty so the Phillies went into the shift with three fielders on the right side of the infield. There was only one player on the left side of the infield. Most of the people watching the game knew Damon would try to steal second. Sure enough, he went on the first pitch. The fielder on the left side of the infield went to cover the throw to second, which happened to go to the right side of the base. Damon who slid into second safely all of a sudden bounced up and sprinted to third base, which was void of any fielders. It wasn't even close. He was safe and the Yankees went on to win the game and the World Series. When asked about it after the game, Damon said that since teams have been shifting when Teixeira was up he had been talking about trying this play all year. Damon saw a tendency that teams did and he capitalized on it at the best possible moment, the World Series.

In youth baseball it can be the smallest of tendencies that teams can exploit. I have always taught aggressive baserunning. One of things I always look at is the opposing pitcher's awareness when there are baserunners. They are kids, and many times a pitcher will keep his head down after throwing a pitch called a "ball" that he knew was a strike. If the pitcher doesn't look at the lead runner after he retrieves the ball from the catcher, this can be an opportunity to steal a base.

I teach and keep reinforcing to my pitchers to always look at the lead runner when they retrieve the ball from the catcher as they are walking back to the pitching rubber. If the pitcher has a lapse in concentration, as sure as you are reading this, a coach will exploit that lapse and get a gift base. Always have your pitcher look at the lead runner and teach your pitchers not to get sucked in to throwing behind the lead runner to get another baserunner taking an extra long lead trying to draw the throw. If there are two outs, then have him throw the ball, otherwise look at the lead runner.

**Related Resources:**

Pitching Drills & Techniques

44 Baseball Mistakes & Corrections

Baseball Coaching: A Guide for the Youth Coach & Parent

The 59 Minute Baseball Practice

*Chapter 34*

# Mistake #33
## Hitters Using Heavy Bats

Every year my parents sent me to sleep away camp in upstate New York. My brothers were there so I loved going. To this day, 50 years later, I still have some of my best friends from there. I was usually in one of the best athletic bunks, and softball, basketball, and touch football seemed to be played almost around the clock by my friends and I. One year, there was another bunk that was the equal of our bunk athletically and we met for the first time on the softball field. You would have thought it was the '51 playoff game with the Giants and the Dodgers. All the other camp counselors and campers wanted to see these two groups of 14 and 15 year-olds go at it on the diamond. In this game, we went ahead early. The other team had a player, Norman, who was a friend of mine from home. Twice in a row, Norman, who batted lefty, hit the ball well over our right fielder's head for a home run and a triple. These two shots were two of the longest I've seen hit on that field, including counselors. We played them two or three more times, and Norman was a machine, hitting homeruns and extra base hits over our right fielder's head. We even put on a shift (The Norman Shift), placing our shortstop as a fourth outfielder. It did not matter. Norman was the hot player that summer. He was as tall as me, but was thinner. Growing up I was a big kid. One night after dinner the campers were given "free play". A few campers from my bunk and from Norman's bunk ended up at the softball field taking turns hitting and shagging fly balls. When I got up, I asked Norman if I could use his bat. He obliged. While swinging it on deck, I was amazed at how light his bat was compared to the bat I was using. I got up to the plate (I bat righty) and I started hitting the ball over the left fielder's head with shots I never knew I could hit. Needless to say, Norman's bat was lighter (much lighter) than the one I was using. He wouldn't let me use his bat when we played his bunk again but I used a much lighter camp bat the rest of the summer and I became the "Norman" for our bunk, hitting the softball over the left fielder's head. I learned at a very young age that it is better to have a lighter bat than a heavier bat.

This is one of the biggest mistakes I see yearly. Parents are buying bats that are too heavy for the kids to get around on the ball. As a parent or coach, you can easily learn by watching how the 10, 11 and 12 year-old kids on your team handle the bat and how quickly they get around on the baseball. You will see charts and hear theories about how heavy a bat should be for a particular age or a kid's size.

My own theory is the eye test. Watch to see if the player can get around on the baseball or if he hits it to the opposite field too often. Experiment with bats of different weights. Really take time to observe and you will become just as good as the more experienced coach in determining if a bat is too heavy for a youth player. Parents also should go to their league's web site and see the requirements and size limitations for bats. This changes every year, and even in the middle of the season. Remember that the most expensive bat is not necessarily the best bat for your son or daughter. Sometimes the old wooden bat your neighbor's kid used ten years ago may be the best bat for your son.

Talking about bats, there is situation that comes up each and every year. The first player on your team to hit a home run over the fence will automatically have the best bat on the team. Every kid will want to use it. Try to dissuade kids from using teammates' bats or becoming dependent on one particular bat. I like my kids to have flexibility and to learn to hit with different bats as long as they are not too heavy. In fact, we will have designated batting practices, where players are not allowed to use their own bat. The main point here is that it is better for a player to swing a lighter bat than a heavier bat.

**Related Resources**

Winning Baseball Strategies

Hitting Drills & Techniques

Baserunning & Bunting Drills

44 Baseball Mistakes & Corrections

Baseball Coaching: A Guide for the Youth Coach & Parent

## *Chapter 35*

# Mistake #34
## Batters Ready To Hit Too Early

The next time you go to a baseball game live, observe the on deck circle. I love watching the routine some of the players have. I've seen some players get so involved in their on deck routine, they have to be reminded when it is their turn to bat. They are in another world sometimes, but this is what they do.

Often youth baseball players are ready to hit even when the pitcher is not close to throwing the baseball.

A number of years ago I had a really good athletic 9-year-old on my team, who had real potential in baseball. I brought him up to our major division in what many people thought was a year too soon. This player had talent, a lot of talent, but he did not channel it properly all the time. And this is the type of player I like to have. An athletic player with a lot of potential that I'll have on my team for four years. Eric (not his real name) not only had talent, but he had an intensity like I had never seen before for a 9-year-old kid. If you ever met an adult who is really intense, it is hard to relax and converse with them. I remember the situation. It was a regular season game and Eric was batting. We just had a rain storm so it was somewhat muddy around the infield and the pitcher's mound. The opposing coach told his pitcher to clean out his spikes. A large amount of mud was accumulating from the previous inning. This was the right move by the other coach. As the pitcher was cleaning his spikes, I glanced at Eric. Sure enough, Eric was in the batter's box with his bat up ready to go. Meanwhile, the pitcher was cleaning out his spikes and was not even looking at home plate. I yelled out, "Eric, relax, the pitcher is not even close to pitching." From this situation I learned that young players all too often are holding their batting stance for too long while the pitcher is not even in his wind-up. This is a disadvantage for the batter, especially young batters, because their concentration span is limited. I've seen pitchers in youth baseball games take time to tie their shoes and the batter is still in the box in his intense stance. I've seen umpires with their back turned to the ball field over at the screen getting a new supply of baseballs, and still, the batter is ready to hit. The player is diminishing his chances of hitting the ball. I was taught long ago that "a relaxed hitter is a dangerous hitter."

We've seen it in major league baseball a million times when the batter is ready and the pitcher keeps shaking off his catcher. Finally the batter asks the umpire for time out. Once it is acknowledged, he steps put of the batter's box to gather himself. Youth players do not have the maturity to realize when their concentration is reaching a limit. I maintain that teaching youth baseball players to relax while hitting may be the best hitting lesson any player will ever have!

From numerous clinics I have attended and books I've read, I developed my own technique for relaxing hitters when waiting for a pitch. I tell my players that if they want to relax (and I leave it up to them) to keep their bat on their shoulders, and once the pitcher starts his wind up they are then to get into their batting stance. Some hitting coaches want the batter to keep the bat parallel to the ground, which is fine. I want my batter to do whatever he needs to be relaxed and get ready once the pitcher begins his wind-up. If a player wants to do what is called the Manny Ramirez - elephant trunk swing with the bat - let him. If he wants to point his bat at the pitcher with one hand, let him do it as long as it is not against the rules.

Of course as the players get older they'll learn that some pitchers will take longer than others. This has to be addressed. The batter may have to get ready sooner or even later. You can do anything you want to teach your hitters to relax, but please keep it simple and don't over coach this part of the game.

**Related Resources:**

Hitting Drills & Techniques

44 Baseball Mistakes & Corrections

Baseball Coaching: A Guide for the Youth Coach & Parent

Infield Team Play & Strategies

Baseball Chronicles: A Guide for the Youth Coach

*Chapter 36*

# Mistake #35

## Batters Stance Consistency After Swing

This mistake with batting is related to the previous one (Players Ready To Hit Too Early). If you watch a lot of baseball games on television, it is fascinating to watch batters get into the batter's box. For those 2-4 minutes they claim the four-foot wide by six-foot long box as their own domain, home or castle. Batter's will dig in, make lines, destroy the lines, and whatever else they can do to make themselves comfortable. They say the key to establishing consistency as a baseball hitter is developing a routine in the batter's box and sticking with it. If the major league batter hits a foul ball or calls time out to gather himself outside the batter's box, when he re-enters the batter's box, his stance is exactly the same as it was before he stepped out. On occasions, the batter will make some adjustments by moving closer or further away from the pitcher, but 95% of the time the major league batter wants to bat the exact same way each and every time. Just like an NBA player who shoots foul shots, he maintains the same form on every foul shot.

I wish it was the same thing in youth baseball. In youth baseball, many times the batter will foul off a ball, swing and miss and go off balance, or step out of the batter's box. When he comes back in, he takes a different stance. This is a mistake! Try teaching players to take the same stance almost all of the time. If the coach is making a recommendation for the batter to adjust his stance, because of a fast throwing pitcher, that is different. Almost every time the batter should get into the same stance.

When talking about the batting stance, there are basically three types. There is the "open stance." The open stance is when the hitter's back foot is closer to home plate than the front foot. The open stance used to be very rare but it has become more popular in recent years at all levels.

The "closed stance" is when the batter's front foot is closer to home plate than the back foot. This stance is not as popular as it used to be.

The "square stance" is when both feet are equal distance from home plate. So if you were to draw a line from one foot to the other and opposite them, it would look like a square.

When talking about which stance to teach youth baseball players, I have my own theory. If it ain't broke, don't fix it. If your player comes to your team with an outer space type of batting stance and is making contact with the baseball, leave him alone. If he becomes a real good player, chances are the parents will give him batting lessons and his instructor will adjust his stance. Why fix something if the player is successful doing it? I remember I was in a sales job and the company had all these instructions about how to make cold calls and how to close the sale and how many calls you have to make a day to be successful. There was one guy in the office and all he did during the week was play golf with people. As he played, he made sales and was the best sales person in the office. The company, for some reason, put a stop to this and kept him in the office with us co-workers. This lasted for two weeks until when he quit and began working for someone else. Why the sales manager would change this person's formula for success is beyond me. It is obvious to me that if you have a winning formula, stay with it.

As coaches we want to encourage players to take the same stance on every pitch. If a young players is lost and needs direction, I like to teach him the square stance and have him set up at one of the points of home plate. Take time during practice and set up a player in the batter's box who is unsure of himself. Play with it a little by changing and tweaking his stance. Like anything else in youth sports, it is repetition and putting players in the position to succeed that make you a successful coach.

**Related Resources:**

<u>Hitting Drills & Techniques</u>

<u>44 Baseball Mistakes & Corrections</u>

<u>Baseball Coaching: A Guide for the Youth Coach & Parent</u>

<u>Baseball Chronicles: A Guide for the Youth Coach</u>

<u>Baseball Chronicles 2: A Guide for the Youth Coach</u>

*Chapter 37*

# Mistake #36
## Not Dropping Bat

One reason why baseball is such a great game is that you are always seeing something new and different over the course of the season. Some things are extremely funny while others raise people's blood pressure to such a point that we forget it is just a game. I've seen players round the bases on a inside the park grand slam only to have the opposing coach think the hitter missed one of the bases. Forgetting who actually hit the ball, he instructed his catcher to go into the dugout and tag everyone in there with the baseball. I've seen a game stopped because a turtle the size of a large pizza entered the playing field at his own pace and the game was delayed 45 minutes until the turtle made it to the other side of the field and under the fence to the stream he came from. Speaking of animals, 3 parents and myself were just about to begin to fix the field after a big rain storm. We started to move a blue tarp in short right field. As we turned over the tarp no less that 10 snakes slithered out. If you never saw 40+ adults run like Olympians, it is quite a site. You will see endless things throughout the baseball season.

When watching a major league baseball game, about once every few games we see a situation when a player hits the ball unexpectedly and has to run if the ball goes fair.

This usually happens when the batter's checks his swing or started to swing and holds up. The ball hits the bat, goes fair, and the batter has to run it out. Usually the ball dribbles right back to the pitcher or to the second baseman. It is a normal part of major league baseball.

I was coaching my middle son's team in what our league called the minor leagues. This league was comprised of players 9 and 10 years-old. We were in a playoff game and had a nice rally going with players on first and second and only one out. The batter up was a little above average in talent and a really good kid. I think the count was something like two balls and two strikes. The next pitch was coming right at my batter's head. He ducked so the baseball would not hit him. While he ducked down, he did not drop the bat and the ball hit the bat and dribbled fair about 3 or 4 feet in front of the pitcher.

No one moved and the home plate umpire, who was experienced did not make a call. I realized then that as odd as the situation looked the ball was in play. Everyone watching the game was focused on the ball going directly for the batter's head and him ducking. I started yelling at my player to run, telling him that the ball was fair. When I yelled, the opposing coach began yelling at his catcher to pick up the ball and throw to first base, which he did. My batter was out, but my two baserunners had the smarts to move to the next base.

When players are batting, and the ball is coming right at them, they must drop or lower their bat when they move or duck away from the ball. This is something most youth coaches don't practice but will tell their players. Remember, and I've said it a million times, you can tell players to do certain things, but if you actually practice and show them how to do it, it is much more effective. You are putting your players in a situation to succeed.

Every year I devote a certain amount of time to practicing how to drop the bat when you have to get out of the way of the ball with each and every player on the team. In fact I simulate what happens when the ball does hit the bat so my team in the field knows they have to field the live baseball. When the ball hits the bat unexpectedly I want my team to already have seen the situation happen before.

This mistake is made by players that I see come up every year. Knowing how to drop the baseball bat should be practiced. It will reinforce to your batters and your fielders what can happen if the ball hits the bat and goes fair.

**Related Resources:**

Hitting Drills & Techniques

44 Baseball Mistakes & Corrections

Baseball Coaching: A Guide for the Youth Coach & Parent

Baseball Chronicles: A Guide for the Youth Coach

Baseball Chronicles 2: A Guide for the Youth Coach

Baserunning & Bunting Drills

*Chapter 38*

# Mistake #37

## Cutting The Batting Swing Short

We have all heard that hitting a baseball is one of the hardest things to do in sports. I've mentioned that when you go to a baseball clinic, it is easy to come away more confused about a skill than when you went in to the clinic. This happens a lot at national clinics that have speakers about hitting. I know there is a need for a lot of this, but when coaching youth baseball most coaches are fully qualified to teach the basics of hitting if they do a little reading at their local library and use their common sense. One of the things I tried to do in my community was to get the high school baseball coach and/or the junior varsity coach to have a hitting clinic for our youth league. I do this because the high school coach usually knows about hitting and will talk about his philosophy. When I set this up for my league I prompted the high school coach and pleaded with him to keep it as simple as possible. The coach I worked with was terrific and we hit it off. This became a yearly tradition. I also like to get the junior varsity coach involved because many times when the youth players my peers and I coach get to high school, the junior varsity coach will become the varsity coach.

As youth coaches, you should become familiar with all the resources available to you. I mentioned books in your local library and seek out as many videos you can.

There are tons of them. Your local batting cage will have some batting instructors. Develop a rapport with them and invite them to hold a clinic and offer that they can distribute discount coupons for hitting lessons.

No matter how much knowledge you have with hitting, you have to keep it as simple as possible. They see many of the same mistakes arise every year. Youth players do not follow through when swinging their bat. I usually notice this with certain batters when the season first begins while we are taking batting practice at the local batting cage. What happens is as odd as it seems. A lot of youth baseball players will stop their swing when they make contact. Now, of course they can't stop their swing at the exact point of making contact, but I've seen some pretty amazing things batters do to try stopping their swing. Can you imagine a golfer trying to stop his swing when he makes contact with the golf ball? Or how about a tennis player stopping his swing on contact on his serve? How an athlete follows through after the point of contact will greatly determine how the ball moves. When youth baseball players stop their swing, they are not following through the right way. Most hitting coaches will talk about bat speed and the need to increase bat speed. In the case of a player not swinging the bat through the ball, he is just hurting himself. As I mentioned, as youth coaches, focus on the basic fundamentals. Don't worry too much about things like one hand or two hand release of the bat. If a player is not following through, or is stopping his bat on contact, there are drills you can do to help correct this.

To help correct this mistake I love to use the batting tee. There are a few types of drills to do off the tee. A good drill is the soccer ball hit. What I do is place a soccer ball on a batting tee. To help keep the ball balanced, buy a small bathroom plunger and turn it upside down in the tee so the ball will sit firmly in the cup part of the plunger. I have the player hit the soccer ball off the tee. I tell him to swing hard and swing right through the soccer ball. This effective drill will help the batter follow through on his swing.

Reinforce to your players who stop their swing to hit through the ball. It is the constant repetition over a period of time that will change bad habits into good habits.

**Related Resources:**

Hitting Drills & Techniques

44 Baseball Mistakes & Corrections

Baseball Coaching: A Guide for the Youth Coach & Parent

The 59 Minute Baseball Practice

Baseball Chronicles 2: A Guide for the Youth Coach

*Chapter 39*

# Mistake #38

## Batter Over Striding And Stepping To Third Base

When youth players are batting, their stride or the movement of the front foot is very important. Lately, many professionals just lift the front foot, not even striding forward, and they are able to transfer their weight and still hit the baseball. In youth baseball, there are some common mistakes when players take that stride forward. Many times players will take too big of a stride. This can be caused by a few things. One of the most common is that the player's feet are too close together in the stance to start and the natural step is over done and longer than necessary. The other is that youth players, and even some adult coaches, feel that a big stride will help the player get more of his weight behind the baseball, when in fact over striding can diminish the power and also the timing when trying to hit the ball.

If you stand in front of a mirror and take a practice swing with an extraordinary long stride you will feel yourself somewhat off balance. Another interesting factor that I picked up from a hitting coach friend of mine is that when you over stride the head drops more than it should. When hitting a baseball, you don't want to move your head in an excessive manner. Again, give this the mirror test. Now concentrate on how low the head moves when over striding. You will see how the heads drops the longer the stride is.

There are a few ways to correct over striding. You can place a piece of wood or bat 12" (or a comfortable distance) in front of the player's front foot. Knowing the wood is there will keep the player from over striding. The repetitions will turn into muscle memory. This will help solve the problem.

I am a big believer that hitting off the batting tee can solve almost any problem that has to do with hitting. All the tips explained don't have to be done in a batting practice situation, but can be done off a batting tee. You can be creative. Hitting off the tee can be done almost anywhere. I've been using rag balls for years. Every year I would pick up a box of rags from the local hardware store. I would then wrap them into balls with 2" masking tape. These rag balls are great! Once you have them made you can hit into a screen or even a wall. Here's a hint: don't wrap them too tight so they lose any bounce back when they hit the wall. They work great on almost every aspect of hitting off the batting tee.

When you want to instruct hitting, even though the players are 10, 11 and 12, or maybe even younger, as a coach you can feel comfortable explaining to the players why certain things are done in a short explanation. Just don't make it a 90-minute college lecture. Most young players will grasp the concept.

Another one of the biggest mistakes made in youth baseball is when the player steps with his front foot the wrong way. Instead of taking the correct small step toward the pitcher, he will step toward third base. And of course a lefty hitter will step toward 1st base incorrectly.

To remedy this, coaches should work on it in practice. One technique is to take two 2X4's and put them in front and behind the player's feet. Once he knows they are there, he will not step toward 3rd base,, knowing if he does, he will hit the wood. This technique has been very effective for me over the years.

There are always exceptions to every rule. Every once in a while you will see a major league hitter that looks totally off balance, over striding and doing everything wrong, except for consistently hitting the ball. I don't have an explanation. With kids, however, if they look like they are batting totally wrong, tweak it one small step at a time.

My good friend, Bobby Woods, is the best hitting instructor I ever met. Bobby had success developing school players for college and college players for the majors. Bobby always emphasized to me that "a relaxed hitter is a dangerous hitter." Bobby said no matter what a batter is doing correctly, if he is tense this will diminish his chance of success. Bobby maintains he'd rather have a relaxed hitter batting with flaws in his stride or swing than a player with a perfect swing who is overly tense.

**Related Resources:**

Hitting Drills & Techniques

44 Baseball Mistakes & Corrections

Baseball Coaching: A Guide for the Youth Coach & Parent

The 59 Minute Baseball Practice

Baseball Chronicles 2: A Guide for the Youth Coach

Baserunning and Bunting Drills

*Chapter 40*

# Mistake #39
## Moving Back Foot While Hitting

If you look at some film clips of Babe Ruth early in his career, he would move up in the box with both feet as the ball was coming to home plate. I'm not sure when and why he changed, but he hit a ton when his back foot was stationary.

It is common in youth baseball for players to move their back foot when instead it should have limited to no movement. Why is this important? It is one of those things where you will get many different answers to the same question. I believe the theory that when hitting the weight transfer is very important and will give the batter a fast bat as well as a powerful swing. If the back foot is moving more than necessary the batter may not be able to keep his balance. This will in turn diminish his chance of success. Why do young players develop this habit? One reason may be that they were never taught the correct way to bat. Even some of the better hitters may hit because of their natural talent. Without making hitting a baseball too confusing for young kids, it is our job to finds little ways to make them better hitters. Another reason kids may move their back foot is that many are generally afraid to get hit by the baseball. Their nervousness will be shown in different ways. Unnecessary body movements is one way young kids respond, with the potential of getting hit with a baseball and getting hurt. Plain and simple, the extra movements are a sign of insecurity. When people speak publicly and are uncomfortable, you will notice different things with that person. He or she may become fidgety, or even start to sweat profusely. Well, it is the same thing for a youngster and their fear of getting hit by the pitch. I have not only seen fidgety kids when they are nervous, I have also experienced kids that get up to bat and are stiff as a board. They walk into the batter's box looking like Frankenstein and stand their without moving their legs, feet, or bat. This kind of nervousness can be dangerous, because I've seen kids not move even when the baseball is coming right toward their head.

Remember, we have to get the kids to relax. If a player does move his back foot too much, I use the "two brick" drill. I place one brick in front of his back foot and one brick behind his back foot. Knowing the bricks are there, the batter will tend to move his back foot less than what he was doing before. This is similar to the player moving his front foot toward third base when swinging. It takes a lot of repetitions to overcome this habit but the two brick drill does work.

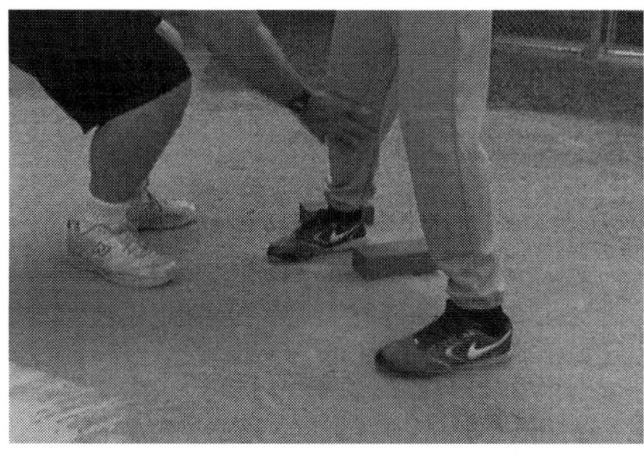

Another good drill to overcome back foot movement is to use a batting tee. Have the batter get into his regular batting stance, but instead of having him step with his front foot like he normally does, have him take an extra high leg kick. On the way down, he hits the ball off the batting tee. Lifting the front foot high will make it almost impossible for the batter to move his back foot more than he has to. This is done to condition his mind not to move the back foot.

With both these drills, the key is to give the player enough repetitions so it becomes normal for the batter to keep his back foot still. I would go from the batting tee to the soft toss (rag balls can be used) to live pitching. If the players falls back into the bad habits, go back on the batting tee. It takes time and does not happen over night. Remember that all kids are different and some kids will grasp changes quicker than others. The key for youth baseball coaches is to give them a chance to change their bad habits into good ones.

**Related Resources:**

Hitting Drills & Techniques

44 Baseball Mistakes & Corrections

Baseball Coaching: A Guide for the Youth Coach & Parent

The 59 Minute Baseball Practice

Baseball Chronicles 2: A Guide for the Youth Coach

Baserunning and Bunting Drills

*Chapter 41*

# Mistake #40
## Taking The Eye Off The Ball While Batting And Fielding

Imagine a surgeon performing surgery and turning his head every few moments. Or how about an auto mechanic taking apart an engine and closing his eyes for seconds at a time. In both cases, the task at hand would seem almost impossible to accomplish unless their eyes were 100% focused on what they had to do. In baseball, it is similar when a young player does not keep his eyes on the ball from when it leaves the pitcher's hand until it reaches home plate. Many times youth baseball players will turn their heads right at the moment of contact. Another example is when a young player is fielding a ground ball. Many times he will take his eye off the baseball just before it is about to go into his glove. This is especially true when a fielder is about to field a grounder for a sure double play. He hurries to get the out, lifts his head, and the baseball goes right under his glove. On the double play error that happens a lot, I instruct my team that the first fielder to field the ball should concentrate on getting one out. Inevitably in their angst to get two, the first player to field the ground ball gets no outs as he moves his head and takes his eye off the baseball. This is a common problem with young players, both in hitting a baseball and fielding a baseball. Taking one's eyes off the baseball is a big mistake youth baseball players make. How do we get young players to overcome this? I will give you a few drills that will help train young baseball players to keep their eyes on the ball.

With hitting, a simple drill utilizes the batting tee. I am a firm believer youth players should spend time every day on the batting tee. When the player makes contact with the baseball on the batting tee, he has to yell out "hit". This will help force him to keep his eyes on the baseball. You can also color code balls with small dots and the player has to yell out the color of the dot upon contact.

Here is another drill,which is a variation of the previous drill, and is one of my favorites. Take three baseballs and color code them with painter's tape. But, not a lot of tape. The batter has to track the baseballs and follow them into the catcher's glove. As soon as he can distinguish the color, he will yell it out. If the three colors are white, yellow, and blue, the batter will yell out one of these colors. A more advanced version of this drill is to have the batter yell out the color when he swings the bat. This drill has the player focus hard on the ball. In turn, he will keep his eye on it.

Here is another advanced toss hitting drill that will help train players to force their eye to stay on the baseball. Use two colored soft covered balls, or two different colored rag balls, toss them up and yell out quickly which ball (or rag ball) you want the player to hit. For instance, if you are using two different colored rag balls, say red and blue, toss them both up at the same time. Then yell out "blue". The player must hit the blue colored rag ball. Kids love this drill, and for some of your advanced hitters you can actually wait longer to call out one of the colors.

For fielding, I use the three colored balls and hit grounders to players in the infield. They must watch the baseball go into their glove and yell out the color as soon as they recognize it. The key here is two-fold; first recognizing which color the baseball is, and then following the baseball into the player's glove.

Keeping the eye on the ball for young players is one of the biggest challenges for coaches and parents. I have seen big programs marketed to help improve eye sight for athletes. Whether these programs work or not I'm not sure. But I am sure of the drills that I just presented will help your players focus on the ball and be more successful hitting and fielding.

**Related Resources:**

Hitting Drills & Techniques

44 Baseball Mistakes & Corrections

Baseball Coaching: A Guide for the Youth Coach & Parent

The 59 Minute Baseball Practice

Drills & Techniques for Catchers

Infield Team Play & Strategies

Fielding Drills & Techniques

*Chapter 42*

# Mistake #41
## Bunting At High Pitches/ Importance Of Bunting

As a coach, I love playing small ball, and a big part of small ball is bunting. In fact, if someone tells me my knowledge about hitting and pitching in baseball is limited, they won't get an argument from me. But, if they tell me I know nothing about bunting and baserunning, I will fight them forever! I have separated the next two mistakes when it comes to bunting, and there is a reason for it. First, let me tell you why I love bunting. Even though many times I will look past certain fundamentals, as long as the kids are enjoying and learning the game, I find that the art of bunting and defending the bunt brings a ton of things into play in baseball. In this section, I will talk about one of the biggest mistakes kids do when bunting, but first here is why I teach bunting. If there is one part of coaching baseball that I may over coach, bunting is it.

I find that even when my opposition knows my batter is bunting, if executed correctly, it is almost impossible to defend. Let's break that down. Suppose there is a runner at first base and it is a close game toward the end of the game. I have a player who is a good bunter up at bat. The righty batter will square to bunt when the pitcher begins to bring his front foot down in his wind up. He will bunt with either the square bunt technique or the pivot bunt (my preference) technique. I teach my players to bunt the ball toward third base in such a way it will be close to the line. If the first bounce is on the dirt around home plate, this is good, but not completely necessary. Upon seeing my batter squaring to bunt, the third baseman will begin to rush to home plate to field the ball. The batter makes contact with the ball, and if done correctly, it will go toward the third base line where the third baseman, not the pitcher or catcher, will field the ball. Remember, the third baseman is rushing in, and in many cases in youth baseball, he is overdoing it. With his momentum going toward home, he must bend down, pick up the ball cleanly, plant his foot, and make an accurate throw to first base, which is off from the direction he is rushing in. Even with below average speed, if the batter puts down a good bunt, I believe the odds are in his favor that he will be safe at first base. Of course, this is not fool proof, but good bunters are safe more times than they are out in youth baseball. When you teach bunting over the course of the season, youth players learn good fundamentals.

When I am in the third base coaching box and give the batter the bunt sign it means that the batter has to bunt at the next pitch. NO NO NO! When giving the bunt sign it means the player should bunt only at buntable balls. Buntable balls means in the strike zone, or in the zone that is comfortable for the batter to lay down a successful bunt. I've given the bunt sign and seen youth players bunt at balls out of the strike zone above their shoulders. Bunting at high pitches is almost an impossible thing to do successfully. Remember that young players are always trying to please their coach.

How do you correct players from bunting at high pitches? When I run my batting practice I always have the batter bunt the first two pitches. I do this for a couple of reasons. First I set up two cones on the third base line about 4 feet apart. If the bunt goes between the two cones they get an extra regular batting practice swing. This is a great method for players to improve their bunting. The second reason is on the bunts I will pitch the ball out of the strike zone. I tell the players they cannot bunt at the balls that are too high or too low. This is teaching the batter discipline and he gets used to pulling his bat back and not bunting at it. Over the course of the season this techniques works.

If you become a coach who bunts a lot like me, here is a hint about a mistake I once made. I had one player, Andrew, who was the best bunter I ever had. He had excellent technique and above average speed. His bunts would literally hug the third base line and die at the perfect moment. Here is the mistake I made. I had Andrew bunting almost every other time he was up. I pulled his dad aside and told him I have to let Andrew swing away more. It is not fair if he bunts almost every time up. At first his father disagreed because he loved seeing his son on base all the time. As the season went on, he agreed it was a good idea. Making him a well rounded hitter was the benefit.

Teach bunting to your team and explain the importance of bunting, but teach them not to bunt at high pitches.

**Related Resources:**

Baserunning and Bunting Drills

Hitting Drills & Techniques

44 Baseball Mistakes & Corrections

<u>Baseball Coaching: A Guide for the Youth Coach & Parent</u>

<u>The 59 Minute Baseball Practice</u>

*Chapter 43*

# Mistake #42
## Bunting At Low Pitches/ Importance Of Fielding Bunts

Years ago there was a player on the New York Yankees who was a great lead off hitter. He made the All Star team and was a great base stealer. I remember once in spring training he was hanging around the batting cage taking turns swinging. One coach yelled to the player, "Let's practice some bunting."

The player responded, "Why should I practice bunting? I never bunt." Being an old time fan, one of the best bunters I ever saw was Mickey Mantle. He was an incredible drag bunter when he batted lefty.

In the previous section I explained how I love teaching my team to bunt. I also love teaching my team to defend the bunt. When my team is defending the bunt I teach them in the clearest and simplest of terms what to do while also communicating with each other. I always have my third baseman in close, and I always yell so my team, the opposing team, and coach hear me say, "Watch out for the bunt."

When the batter squares, my third baseman runs in. I teach most of my players to yell bunt. I teach my third baseman that if the batter pulls back, stop where he is and get into his fielding stance. If the batter does bunt, I do want my 3rd baseman fielding the ball because we have practiced it this way. If he is fielding a ball that is not moving, it is important to pick it up bare handed. This saves time instead of the fielders picking the ball up with his glove and then pulling it out. He should plant his foot and throw to the first baseman, who is giving him a good target. I rarely have my first baseman charge for the bunt, just because many youth coaches don't teach their team to bunt toward 1st base. Here is an important hint for all coaches. Make sure your right fielder runs over toward the foul line to line himself up with the 3rd baseman fielding the bunt and then move toward the infield, but not too close. Teaching this back-up will pay tons of dividends for your team over the course of a season. I can't tell you how many times throughout my 25 years of coaching that my right fielder has saved an extra base by backing up the throw.

Just as it is a huge mistake to bunt at high pitches, it is a mistake to bunt at low pitches. Young players will do this by sticking out their bat and tilting it downward toward the ball, almost pointing it down to the dirt .

When the barrel is lower than the handle it is almost impossible to bunt the ball fair. I teach my players on a low strike that they must bend their knees to bunt the baseball correctly. When I teach bunting I'm always teaching my players to keep the bat barrel a little higher than the handle.

Like in the previous mistake of bunting at high pitches, the best way to correct this is to throw pitches out of the strike zone purposely and have your players pull the bat back. Bat discipline is important to teach, even when young players are anxious to get the job done for their coach and or parents.

Some players that receive the bunt sign when they are in the batter's box think they have to bunt at the next pitch.  This is another huge mistake. Relate to them how in football many times the play called in the huddle is different from the play that is actually run. The quarterback calls a lot of audibles. Emphasize to your team that when they get the bunt sign they are only allowed to bunt at buntable balls. They are not to bunt at balls that are too high or too low. Bunts are a huge part of baseball if used at the correct time with the correct technique.

**Related Resources:**

44 Baseball Mistakes & Corrections

Baseball Coaching: A Guide for the Youth Coach & Parent

The 59 Minute Baseball Practice

Baserunning and Bunting Drills

Fielding Drills & Techniques

*Chapter 44*

# Mistake #43
## Eye Test

One of my favorite stories in sports occurred in 1969. Vince Lombardi was one of the greatest football coaches of all time. He was legendary when he coached in Green Bay. After retiring as head coach, Lombardi came back in 1969 to coach the Washington Redskins. The team had drafted a college blocking back named Larry Brown from Kansas State in the 8th round. There was something special about Brown that Coach Lombardi saw. He did well in practice, but Lombardi thought something was missing when he hit the hole from the backfield. Lombardi determined that Brown was getting off the snap count a little late. Vince Lombardi determined that Larry Brown had a hearing problem in one ear. He demanded he take an extensive hearing test and this proved Lombardi correct. The Redskins lobbied the NFL league office for permission to allow Brown to have a hearing piece fitted in his helmet on the side of his weak ear to hear quarterback Sonny Jurgensen's snap counts. After receiving permission Larry Brown was a different back. He hit the hole almost as quick as any back that Vince Lombardi coached.

Larry Brown went on to play in 4 Pro-bowls and play in the Super Bowl. And to think that if coach Vince Lombardi never theorized about his lack of hearing in one ear, a great player may have never flourished!

A number of years ago a player on my team was having trouble hitting the baseball. This player was an above average player, who in fact was my best pitcher, but he was striking out at an alarming rate. I was doing the best I could giving him hints and even suggesting he try a different bat. Nothing was working. In fact, he hit better as an eleven year old than as a twelve year old. His father was my assistant coach and we both discussed this and decided to give him extra help. We went down to the field on a Sunday morning with a bucket of practice baseballs. He was hitting better, but there was something radically wrong that I just could not put my finger on it. During a break, I asked Johnny if he has trouble seeing the blackboard at school when he is in the back of the room. He said yes, and confirmed what I suspected. His vision had gotten worse. I asked his father to have him get an eye test. He agreed and he ended up getting contact lenses. He was a different hitter the second half of the year.

Another year I had Skip, a big first baseman, who hit his share of home runs during the season. He played first base, and played it well. Then he started to commit errors at first. I mean easy throws that his glove was nowhere near the baseball. I then went through the scorebook and noticed the errors he was making were all at night games. I asked Skip's parents to do the same as Johnny and get an eye test. Sure enough he needed glasses because of a stigma for darkness. After he got the glasses, he too was a different ball player. He started to blast home runs every other time up and he never made another error that season.

Now, I'm in no way comparing myself to Vince Lombardi, but as coaches we have to notice details and theorize about different things. Why is this kid not hearing me? Why is this good athlete striking out? Is the bat too heavy? Is the bat too light? Does he need a hearing test or eye test? I'm not saying to become a psychologist or doctor, but take notice of things that might be considered outside the box.

I run my parents meeting about three months before the season starts. On my handout, which is only about three pages long, I have a form asking when their son or daughter had their last hearing and eye test. I urge all coaches to do this. I've experienced this situation twice where getting glasses or contacts for one of my players changed the way he played the game. A great way to explain this to the parents is to tell them my story. It is 100% true!

**Related Resources:**

Hitting Drills & Techniques

44 Baseball Mistakes & Corrections

Baseball Coaching: A Guide for the Youth Coach & Parent

The 59 Minute Baseball Practice

Baseball Chronicles 2: A Guide for the Youth Coach

*Chapter 45*

# Mistake #44
## Coaches Over Coach

I went over to another field to scout an All Star game in which we were playing the winners. I took my normal viewing spot, which is usually along the first or third base line. When this game took place it was way before the cell phone revolution and there were not any rules against having electronic devices in the dugout. It only took me a few minutes to realize that the team in the field had what it seemed like coaches all over the place in foul territory. Actually there was about three in total, but what made them stand out was that each of them was either holding or talking into a walkie-talkie. I looked into the dugout and saw the manager holding his own walkie-talkie talking to one of his assistant coaches. Then after each pitch, he would adjust one or more of the fielders moving them left, right, in, or further out. I thought how ridiculous these wannabe "Billy Martins" were taking their coaching responsibilities. In my mine it was beyond comprehension. This was one of the worst examples of over coaching I ever witnessed.

I've seen it for years. I'm not saying it is right, and I'm not saying it is wrong. I have my own theories, and teaching techniques for kids 8-12 years-old. I'm not saying I'm the best youth coach in the world. But, after coaching for 25 years, running over 1,000 practices, and coaching about 500 games, I have an idea of what works to motivate kids. I'm not right all the time, and am still learning. You will have to become more flexible than you may want if you coach any youth sports over a long period of time. You have to find your own comfort zone as a coach or a parent. Most youth sports coaches, whether they admit it or not, will sometimes over coach their team. Some overzealous coaches will over coach too much.

I have certain rules I adhere to so structurally as I try not over coach. An example is when one of my players is in the batter's box. I have had a few confrontations with parents instructing their own kids when they are batting. Move up in the box, move back in the box. Put your elbow up. Put your elbow down. Instructions like this will usually diminish most youth player's chances of being successful. The reason being is that the coaching and teaching aspect of sports has to be done during practices. When my batters bat I want them to be as relaxed as possible. I don't want my players confused or thinking about too many things in the batter's box. This is part of the parent's meeting I run at the beginning of the season. I tell them not to instruct their own kids when they are batting. I've had confrontations with a dialogue like this:

Mr. Peters: Eric, move up in the box just like you were taught and remember not to take too big a step.

Coach Marty: Mr. Peters, remember what we went over in the parents meeting. Let's give Eric the best chance to hit on his own.

Mr. Peters: What, now you're telling me I can't instruct my own kid? And after spending $2,000. on hitting instructions. Are you serious?

Coach Marty: Hey Mr. Peters, no one wants to have Eric succeed more than me. And the batting instruction he gets is good, but we both have to know when to instruct and when I'll have to have you removed from the field. I've done it before and I won't hesitate to do it again."

This may sound harsh but it is effective.

Another example of over coaching is the 1st and 3rd situation in youth baseball. I have known coaches that have up to 12 different plays to defend this. Remember who you are coaching. This is way too extreme. It reminds me years ago of a professional football offensive coordinator who was fired. In the press conference with the newly appointed offensive coordinator the first question asked is what is the first thing he is going to do?

He answered saying he will cut the playbook in half. He thought it was too complicated. He in fact cut it to a third of what it was and the team went from be a losing team to being a winning team.

Remember what I have been saying throughout this book. Don't feed your players with too much information at one time. Not all of them, but many, will not absorb all of it. Pace yourself throughout the season. Coaches and parents can teach the way they want to teach. I recommend for coaches to keep it more simple than complicated and practice. The more things young kids have to think about in the course of a game, the less likely they will be in a position to succeed.

**Related Resources:**

44 Baseball Mistakes & Corrections

Baseball Coaching: A Guide for the Youth Coach & Parent

The 59 Minute Baseball Practice

Baseball Chronicles 2: A Guide for the Youth Coach

Baserunning and Bunting Drills

# Marty Schupak's Coaching Resources

## *Baseball Videos*

T-Ball Skills & Drills
The 59 Minute Baseball Practice
Backyard Baseball Drills
Pitching Drills & Techniques
Hitting Drills & Techniques
Baserunning & Bunting Drills
Drills & Techniques For The Catcher
Fielding Drills & Techniques
Infield Team Play & Strategies
44 Baseball Mistakes & Corrections
Advanced Toss & Batting Tee Drills

## *Baseball Books*

Baseball Coaching: A Guide For The Youth Coach & Parent ebook
Baseball Chronicles 1: Articles On Youth Baseball
Baseball Chronicles 2: Articles On Youth Baseball
Youth Baseball Drills
44 Baseball Mistakes & Corrections

## *Other Sports Products By Marty Schupak*

*VIDEOS*

48 Championship Basketball Drills
Driveway Basketball Drills
Offensive Basketball Moves
Basketball Fundamentals
Championship Soccer Drills
Backyard Soccer Drills
34 Soccer Goalie Drills
Soccer Shooting Drills
Soccer Fast Footwork Drills
Advanced Soccer Drills
Backyard Golf
Championship Hockey Drills
Backyard Lacrosse

*BOOKS*

Basketball Chronicles: Articles on Youth Coaching
Soccer Chronicles: Articles on Youth Coaching
Sports Chronicles (Baseball, Basketball, & Soccer): Articles on Youth Coaching

CLIFF VERMONT SERIES (Young Adult)

Playoff Fever & Split Pants
Shoot the Pill & Smashed Puzzle

I have tried to make all of my products available for free. All of my videos are free on Amazon Prime. Your library should, and will, carry the DVD format of every one of my videos. You have to ask them. If your library has "Hoopla" my videos are there. All my videos are also available as Apps at the Apple App store, Keyword: Schupak Sports. If your league or recreation department wants a T-Ball clinic, contact us at: www.tballamerica.com.

# Baseball & Softball League Resources

T-Ball America
9 Florence Court
Valley Cottage, NY 10989
Phone: 845-536-4278
www.tballamerica.com

American Amateur Baseball Congress (AABC)
AABC National Headquarters
100 West Broadway, Farmington, NM 87401
Phone: 505-327-3120
Fax: 505-327-3132
Email: aabc@aabc.us
www.aabc.us

Babe Ruth Baseball
PO Box 5000, Trenton, NJ 08638
Phone: 609-695-1434
Fax: 609-695-2505
http://www.baberuthleague.org/

Continental Amateur Baseball Association (CABA)
82 University St, Westerville, OH 43081
Phone: 740-382-4620, 740-382-4620
www.cababaseball.com

Dixie Youth Baseball (DYB)
PO Box 1778, Marshall, TX 75671
Phone: 903-927-1845
Fax: 903-927-1846
Email: boys@dixie.org
www.dixie.org

Dizzy Dean Baseball, Inc.
2470 Hwy 51 S, Hernando MS 38632
Phone: 662-429-4365, 662-429-7790
Email: dizzydeanbaseball@yahoo.com
http://dizzydeanbbinc.org/

Hap Dumont Youth Baseball (National Baseball Congress)
PO Box 17455, Wichita, KS 67217
Phone: 316-721-1779, 316-838-1467
Fax 316-721-8054
Email: hapdumontbball@yahoo.com
www.hapdumontbaseball.com

Little League® International
539 U.S. 15
Williamsport, PA 17702
(570) 326-1921
www.littleleague.org/

National Amateur Baseball Federation (NABF)
PO Box 705, Bowie MD 20715
Phone: 301-464-5460, 301-352-0214,
Fax 301-352-0214
Email: nabf1914@aol.com
www.nabf.com

National Association of Police Athletic Leagues (NPAL)
658 West Indiantown Road, #201, Jupiter, FL 33458
Phone: 561-745-5535
Fax 561-745-3147
Email: copnkid1@aol.com
www.nationalpal.org

PONY Baseball, Inc.PONY Baseball, Inc.
PO Box 225, Washington, PA 15301
Phone: 724-225-1060
Fax: 724-225-9852
Email: pony@pulsenet.com
www.pony.org

T-Ball USA
2499 Main St, Stratford, CT 06615
Phone: 203-381-1449
Fax: 203-381-1440
Email: teeballusa@aol.com
www.teeballusa.org

USA Baseball
403 Blackwell St. Durham, NC 27701
Phone: 919-474-8721
Fax: 919-474-8822
Email: usabasebal@aol.com
www.usabaseball.com

United States Amateur Baseball Association (USABA)
PO Box 55633, Seattle, WA 98155
Phone: 425-776-7130
Fax: 425-776-7130
Email: usaba@usaba.com
www.usaba.com

## ABOUT THE AUTHOR

Marty Schupak has been coaching baseball for 25 years. He has coached over 1,400 kids in youth athletics in a variety of sports along with baseball. Many of his former players have gone on to play in high school and beyond. Many have received athletic college scholarships. Besides coaching baseball, Schupak has coached children in basketball and soccer. He has served on many leagues' boards of directors and is a member of the American Baseball Coaches Association. Thousands of youth baseball coaches have been trained at his clinic, How to Run a Youth Baseball Practice. He is the founder and president of the Youth Sports Club, a group dedicated to improving coaching and youth baseball practices. His website, YouthSportsClub.com, is one of the most popular resources for youth coaches and parents.

He is the creator of eleven baseball videos including: The 59 Minute Baseball Practice, Backyard Baseball Drills, Winning Baseball Strategies, Hitting Drills & Techniques, and seven others. He is also the creator of thirteen videos in other sports including the best selling 48 Championship Basketball Drills. He is also the author of numerous books including the popular book Youth Baseball Drills and the e-book: Baseball Coaching: A Guide for the Youth Coach and Parent, as well as Baseball Chronicles. He also is the author of the Cliff Vermont book series including the popular Playoff Fever & Split Pants. He is the developer of the Baseball PakPad™ and the iSports Universe iPhone applications.

He received a bachelor's degree from Boston University in 1975 and a master's degree in physical education from Arizona State University in 1978. Schupak lives in Valley Cottage, New York.

67296283R00089



Made in the USA
Charleston, SC
08 February 2017